Please return/renew this item by the last date shown.
Items may also be renewed by the internet*

https://library.eastriding.gov.uk

* Please note a PIN will be required to access this service
  - this can be obtained from your library

'Funny. Profound. Moving. Truthful. Rob tells stories that make you laugh, and make you cry, and make you better'
Bob Hartman, author of *The Wolf Who Cried Boy*

'A sparkling collection of tales from years of speaking and writing. Rob doesn't just tell his tales, he invites his readers to become part of the experience'
Adrian Plass, author and speaker

'These stories will stay with you forever. Make sure you're sitting comfortably – you are going to *love* this book!'
Cathy Madavan, author of *Digging for Diamonds*

Let Me
Tell You
A Story

the best of

Rob Parsons

HODDER &
STOUGHTON

First published in Great Britain in 2017 by Hodder & Stoughton
An Hachette UK company

1

Copyright © Rob Parsons, 2017
Illustration © Kuo Kang Chen 2017

A CIP catalogue record for this title is available from the British Library

ISBN 978 1 473 67095 2
eBook ISBN 978 1 473 67098 3

Typeset in Garamond MT by Hewer Text UK Ltd, Edinburgh
Printed and bound in the UK by Clays Ltd, St Ives plc

Hodder & Stoughton policy is to use papers that are natural, renewable
and recyclable products and made from wood grown in sustainable
forests. The logging and manufacturing processes are expected to
conform to the environmental regulations of the country of origin.

Hodder & Stoughton Ltd
Carmelite House
50 Victoria Embankment
London EC4Y 0DZ

www.hodder.co.uk

To the memory of Julie McQuoid, an incredible wife, mother, daughter and friend. She truly was — and is — an inspiration.

Contents

Contents

Acknowledgements

LOOKING BACK OVER the last thirty years, I realise that so many people in Care for the Family have contributed to this book. Whether they have been involved in accounts, admin, marketing, resources, the warehouse, customer care or our various family initiatives, they have all played a part in this charity which has made such a difference in the lives of so many.

Special thanks to Stephen Hayes for his help and, of course, to our senior editor, Sheron Rice.

I am grateful to Ian Metcalfe and his team at Hodder & Stoughton; they have been great, as has my agent Eddie Bell – a legend – and the Bell Moreton Lomax agency.

And, finally, a very special thank you to my wife, Dianne.

Let me introduce you

ROB PARSONS IS the consummate communicator
– writing books, speaking on the radio and TV, and
addressing over a million people at live events throughout
the world. Many of his stories may be familiar to you, as
they are to me and my colleagues at Care for the Family,
the charity Rob founded in 1988. The incredible thing is
that we never tire of hearing these anecdotes amassed
from his personal experiences and those of so many
people from around the world.

As Care for the Family celebrates its thirtieth anniversary, we thought it was the perfect time to ask Rob if he
would let us pick some of our favourite stories for him
to tell once again in this book. After a hectic time scouring
books, zapping back and forth through DVDs, and

unearthing half-forgotten articles, we've put together a wonderful collection. I have had the privilege of working with Rob for over twenty-five years, and I'm thrilled that he agreed to this special project.

Prepare for some laughter and tears, and get ready to be challenged and encouraged as you spend a little time with Rob, the storyteller.

Sheron Rice
Senior Editor at Care for the Family

Around a fire

A COUPLE OF YEARS ago, some friends bought us a fire pit. I'm sure you've seen one: a large metal dish on a stand that you fill with wood and charcoal to enjoy an open fire outside.

On an early September evening last year, we lit the fire pit in our garden and sat huddled around it with some friends. We caught up on news from each other's lives, but mostly just told stories from the past. As those recollections came tumbling out, they were both sad and full of joy. At one moment, we were sombre as we remembered a good friend no longer with us, and the next we were laughing so loudly that I half-feared the neighbours would call the police.

After a while, it started to get a little chilly, so I went indoors to get some blankets. We wrapped them around our shoulders and carried on with our conversation, but as the evening lengthened, people began to shiver. I said to Dianne, 'What on earth are we all doing sitting around this little fire draped in blankets when we've got a perfectly good house back there with central heating?'

We all laughed out loud at the apparent foolishness of it, but I say 'apparent' because deep down we knew it wasn't foolish at all. From the beginning of time, fire has been important to community, and when we gather around one, even in our technological age, we capture something of a sense of oneness. But another element was part of that September evening together – an element as old as fire itself: *stories.* As we hunched around the flames remembering old times, good times, sad times, and above all, people we'd known and loved, we were drawn together in an almost mystical way.

I think Henri Nouwen must have been trying to explain that phenomenon when he wrote:

The word is always a word for others. Words need to be heard. When we give words to what we are living, these words need to be received and responded to. A speaker needs a listener. A writer needs a reader.

When the flesh – the lived human experience – becomes word, community can develop. When we say, 'Let me tell you what we saw. Come and listen to what we did. Sit down and let me explain to you what happened to us. Wait until you hear whom we met', we call people together and make our lives into lives for others. The word brings us together and calls us into community.

I have never lost my wonder at the power of what Nouwen called 'the word' in a simple story. Through all of time and in all kinds of civilisations and cultures, stories have been shared by paupers and kings, with children and the aged, with those who are happy in life and those low in spirit. They are the way we learn to understand the world around us – expressing emotion, passing on wisdom, and bringing people together. Stories and parables explain some of the most complex truths in life.

Let Me Tell You a Story is the culmination of a lifetime of telling stories, and I do hope you enjoy them. Sometimes I have given a word of explanation as to why the story caught my attention, or why I wrote it, but often I have let them speak for themselves. As my mind goes back over the years, I can picture myself looking out into a darkened auditorium and hearing the laughter or feeling the emotion as something I've shared resonates in someone's heart.

Henri Nouwen is right when he says that 'a speaker needs a listener', so *Let Me Tell You a Story* is, in some ways, my expression of gratitude to all of you who have listened to my stories over the years. I have loved telling them to you. Thank you for that privilege.

The first time I told this story, I could tell it was very special. From the moment the opening sentence left my lips, I sensed a resonance throughout the audience, and that is still true when I tell it today. I think it's because the truth in this story is not limited to a moment or a place in time: universally, people want to know that genuine love can rise above the fleeting fragility of appearances, to know that love can be anchored in memories, perseverance and commitment. It's my favourite love story.

My favourite love story

JOHN BLANDFORD WAS in a library in New York just before the outbreak of the last world war. He was flicking through the pages of a book and in the margin he saw some notes in what looked like a woman's handwriting. Sure enough, when he turned to the flyleaf there was a woman's name and address: Hollis Meynell.

John was intrigued by what she'd written and so he wrote to Hollis Meynell. She wrote back, and then he was called to the war in Europe. But they continued to correspond and after a few months he found that he was getting attracted to Hollis, so when he next wrote he said, 'Please would you send me a photograph. I'd like to see what you look like.'

'No, no,' she said. 'If you really care for me, it shouldn't matter what I look like.'

Well, he found that rather hard, but they kept writing. After six months or so it seemed that she had some affection for him and that gave him the courage to ask the question again, 'Would you send me a photograph?'

'No, no,' she said. 'If you really care for me, it shouldn't matter what I look like.'

After eleven months, John was due for his first furlough and he wrote to Hollis saying, 'I'm coming home at Christmas. Will you meet me?'

She said, 'I will – 6.00 p.m. on Christmas Eve at Grand Central Station, New York.'

'How will I recognise you?' he asked.

She wrote back, 'I'll wear a red rose in my right lapel. And how will I recognise *you*?'

He said, 'Well, I'll be in my uniform, but I tell you what: I'll hold the book you wrote the notes in high above my head.'

Well, imagine it. He is quite in love with this woman he has never seen. Let John Blandford take up the story:

Finally, the day came. I walk into Grand Central Station. There are hundreds of people milling around, I am searching for this woman who has captured my heart, and suddenly, out of the crowd steps a young woman. She has long fair hair and is dressed in green. It seemed as if springtime was bursting out of her. I was captivated – so captivated I omitted to notice that she was not wearing a rose. She smiled at me, she jiggled her hips, and as she walked by she looked back and said, 'Going my way, soldier?'

I was about to follow her but suddenly, out of the corner of my eye, I saw the woman wearing the rose. She was older – much older – than I had thought she would be. She had a little knitted hat on to keep out the cold and a long brown overcoat that made its way down to sensible flat brown shoes. She wore little round glasses and carried a silver-tipped cane.

I desperately wanted to go after the young woman in green but then I thought, 'No, this lady has sustained me through the long months of the war. This won't be romance, but it might be something deeper.' I did not hesitate. I walked up to the woman with the rose and said, 'My name is John Blandford; you must be Hollis Meynell. Could I take you to dinner?'

The elderly lady half smiled, half scowled. 'Young man,' she said, 'I have no idea what all this is about, but the young woman in green who just went by begged me to wear this rose. And she said that if you were to invite me to dinner she'll be waiting for you in the big restaurant across the road. Apparently, young man, it was some kind of test.'[1]

As I think back on that story I realise that Hollis Meynell was bright – very bright. She knew that one day even *her* great looks would fade. She was looking for a man who could, at least at some level, love unconditionally. But this is not just Hollis's quest; it is the great search of all our hearts as human beings. We know the world will love us if we are attractive and successful, but whether we are or not, is there anybody who will love us – *anyway*?

We all have dreams. Some of us have seen a dream fulfilled, others have seen a hope dashed. But what of those whose fear of failure has kept them from even beginning — attempting — their dream?

Dreams and fears

ON A TRIP to the Middle East, I spent a few minutes watching a camel owner offering rides to tourists. Giggling teenagers bounced along, ageing bodies held grimly on to the reins, and to the delight of the watching crowd, one super-cool thirty-something went flying over the beast's head! But my main memory is of a small boy. He could have been no more than five years old. A little earlier, his father had led him and his older sister over to see the camel at close quarters. The animal towered above them, occasionally showing teeth that made the wolf in *Red Riding Hood* look positively gummy. The worldly-wise sibling, who was all of ten, had confidently stroked the camel, while her brother poked a hand out nervously towards it from behind his father's back.

Now it was the big moment, and he and his sister had the chance to ride the camel. The boy watched wide-eyed as his sister was lifted onto its back. As she began her short journey, he ran out from behind his father and waved at his sister, laughing loudly. He was totally captivated, enjoying every moment, but then, as the camel turned to come back, I could see his small face change as an awful reality dawned on him: it was his turn next.

He ran straight back behind his father and no amount of cajoling from either father or camel owner would get him anywhere near the animal. Finally, the dad gave up, paid for his daughter's ride, took both children's hands and started off down the street. And it was when they had gone ten metres that I saw something that moved me greatly: the small boy stopped, turned, looked wistfully back at the camel and then continued down the road. That look conveyed what he couldn't say: 'I desperately want to try . . . but I just can't.'

I have seen that look so often in the eyes of not children, but adults. I have sometimes felt it in my own spirit. It is a look that gazes at an opportunity, that caresses a dream, that imagines a relationship – but is paralysed by fear.

There's an incredible poster of Taylor Knox, a surfer, in front of a huge wave (over fifty feet high!) at Todos Santos in Mexico. Underneath are the words, 'What if your fears and dreams existed in the same place?' I think that by nature I can be a fearful person and especially, perhaps, allow the fear of failure to hold me back.

Theodore Roosevelt put it like this:

It is not the critic who counts . . . The credit belongs to the man who is actually in the arena, whose face is marred by dust and sweat and blood . . . who at the best knows in the end the triumph of high achievement, and who at the worst, if he fails, at least fails while daring greatly, so that his place shall never be with those cold and timid souls who know neither victory nor defeat.

As I think of these things, I imagine a small boy suddenly stopping in a dusty street and turning to yell at an old man leading a camel: 'Hey, mister! I've changed my mind!'

When I was a boy, there wasn't a great deal of money in our home. My mother wasn't academic; she could read and write but not a great deal more than that. However, she was good with money. She had to be! I wrote the following story based on what I saw my mother do when I was a child. When I went into the world of business, I found that people often despised unsophisticated money strategies like hers, yet many multi-national companies could have been saved from disaster by understanding the simple principles that my mother adopted.

The wonder of cash

HERBERT LIVED IN a small village. He worked as a farmhand and every week the farmer gave him £200 in wages. When he brought his money home each Friday, Herbert and Alice, his wife, would spread the money out on the table in piles of £10 notes and then they would begin to plan how they would spend it. Alice had never passed an examination; nevertheless, she was very good with money and she used what she called her cup bank. Every week she put different-coloured cups on the table, each one carefully labelled.

First, she would put £80 in the cup marked 'Rent'. The collector called every Saturday morning and he had never been disappointed. Next, she put £60 in the cup marked 'Food'. There were cups for 'Gas', 'Electricity', 'Clothes',

'Insurance', 'Holidays', 'Council Tax' and a few others. When bills had to be paid monthly or even yearly, Alice would work out how much they needed to put in the cup each week so that there would be enough in it by the time the payment was due. And finally, Alice would put whatever was left in the 'Savings' cup. There was rarely more than £20 spare to put in there. Some weeks she found there was more money than she needed in one of the cups, and when that happened she put it into her 'Rainy Day' teapot, where it built up over the years.

It is true that Herbert and Alice had few luxuries, but if you had asked them whether they were poor, they would have smiled and said, 'Of course, not. We have a warm house, plenty of food, holidays, and we save a little.' And then they would have added, 'We don't have any debts.'

One day, their next-door neighbour, Clarence, called in to see them. He was a foreman on a nearby farm and earned twice as much as Herbert. When he called, they were dividing Herbert's wages up as they did every week, the cups lined up across the kitchen table. Clarence asked what was happening and when they told him he laughed out loud.

'You're so unsophisticated,' he exclaimed. 'And foolish! You shouldn't leave your precious money in those silly cups – it ought to be in a bank earning interest.'

Herbert felt stung that he and Alice had been so foolish. 'How much interest does your money earn, Clarence?' he asked.

'Two per cent!' Clarence replied proudly.

The next day Herbert met Clarence in the street and asked if he would help him look after his money in a better way. 'Delighted!' said Clarence. 'Meet me in the pub on Tuesday night!'

'But don't tell Alice,' Herbert urged.

'Mum's the word!' shouted Clarence, tapping his nose.

Herbert sat wide-eyed as Clarence explained what sophisticated people did with their money. He felt embarrassed that he had let Alice, who obviously didn't have a clue about finance, look after their affairs. Clarence told him that clever people put all their money in a bank and then, instead of cash, the bank gave them a piece of plastic to use. It was practically magic. All the shops seemed to prefer it to cash, but if you ever needed any readies you could put the plastic in a hole in the wall and real money would come out. The bank paid you interest on any money you didn't use and it just built up and up.

It sounded too good to be true.

'Has anybody ever stolen your card, Clarence, and bought things for themselves using your money?'

'Yes, plenty of times. In fact, somebody once went to the trouble of actually making a card just like mine and using it. But it's no problem. You just tell the bank and they normally give you all the money back.'

'What do you mean by *normally*, Clarence?'

'Oh, don't worry about that.'

That night Herbert told Alice how he was going to take charge of their financial affairs from then on and, with Clarence's help, get a plastic card that could even give them money from a hole in a wall. Alice had a dreadful feeling that something was wrong, but she didn't argue because she knew that she wasn't clever.

Herbert couldn't wait for his first bank statement to see how much interest his money had made him, and when he heard the postman come, he rushed to the door like he used to do on his birthday when he was a boy. When he saw the figure, he couldn't believe it – seven pence! How could it possibly be true? Alice, who was foolish with money, explained it to him. 'We put £800 in over the month. All our bills came out and just our savings stayed in. On average we accumulated £3 a day earning interest at 2 per cent per annum.'

'Well, it's better than nothing!' said Herbert, 'and better than it was just standing in those cups of yours!'

It was in the third month that things began to go terribly wrong. One day Herbert met Clarence in the street and said, 'Do you sometimes find that you spend more with the card than you used to with cash?'

'I can't remember the cash days, old boy!' Clarence answered. 'Don't worry about it!'

When the statement came at the end of the third month Herbert wasn't anything like as keen to rush to get it. In fact, Alice opened it. Her face went pale. 'It says we've got minus £23 and somebody has taken £20 out of our account. There's a letter as well, but I don't understand it.'

Herbert snatched the statement from her and rushed around to Clarence's house. He caught his neighbour just as he was leaving for a darts match. 'What's happened to my money and who's taken that £20?'

Clarence told Herbert to calm down and explained. 'This month you somehow spent £3 more than you had in your account.'

'But how can I spend money I haven't got?' asked Herbert.

'Well, the bank allowed you to do it by lending you some of their money.'

'But I didn't ask to borrow their money.'

Clarence coughed. 'Well, that's the problem – I should probably have explained it to you – it happens to me all the time. Because you spent more than you had in your account and you hadn't asked the bank to lend you the money, they lent it to you without asking you if you really wanted it. It's what they call an "unauthorised overdraft".'

'Did they want me to borrow it?' asked Herbert.

'No, they were very cross that you did.'

'Then why did they lend it to me?'

'Because you are a good customer,' said Clarence.

'And will they charge me interest?'

Clarence coughed again. 'Well, yes – rather a lot actually. In fact, 27 per cent.'

'And is that the £20 they've taken from my account?'

'Oh no, the interest charge will come next month. That £20 is for the letter they wrote to you telling you you've spent too much. If you don't put it right soon they'll send you another one and charge you again.'

Herbert walked home clutching the bank statement with his head held low. When he got in, Alice was making their supper. 'Alice, I've been foolish,' he said. 'When you put our money in the cups every week we knew how much we had and what we had left. If we didn't have it, we didn't spend it. I felt silly that our money wasn't earning interest, but after just three months at 2 per cent we've only made nineteen pence. And after one mistake, the bank has charged us £20, and next month they are going to charge us 27 per cent on the extra money we borrowed.'

Alice smiled. 'Don't worry, Herbert,' she said. 'It's not your fault. We're just not clever enough to use our money wisely. Next week we'll go back to the cups.'

Herbert felt so relieved. In fact, that night at the pub, he told everybody he met what had happened and how only very clever people could handle their money wisely. He and Alice were going back to their silly cups.

Word of stupid Alice and her cups spread like wildfire. The next day, when Alice opened the door to get the milk, there was a queue of people waiting to see her. She didn't know all of them but she did recognise the man from the library, the teacher and her butcher. The man standing at the front had been there over an hour; he was the local solicitor. 'Are you Stupid Alice?' he asked.

'Yes,' she said, 'that's me.'

'We were wondering if you could show us how to use the cups.'

I have rarely come across a story that has as much power to touch people of all generations as this one, which a friend shared with me over fifteen years ago. When I have told it, people of all ages have been moved. I remember on one occasion, I was speaking at a company's annual conference in front of two hundred of their staff. The managing director, a well-known television celebrity, was sitting in the front row and next to her was her company accountant. He was in his mid-sixties and whereas the others in the room were casually dressed, he wore a three-piece pinstriped suit and a collar and tie. For most of my talk he'd looked pretty bored, but as I neared the end of this story I saw his demeanour change. He leant forward, listening eagerly, and then, as I spoke the very last sentence, he took out a handkerchief and quickly brushed away a tear.

Information please

PAUL WAS A little boy whose parents owned one of the first telephones. They lived on the plains in America, and the wooden box with a handle was installed in their farmhouse kitchen. He thought it was a wonderful machine. His mother would wind it up and say, 'Information please,' and a lady would reply, 'This is Information.' It was incredible. Information Please would get them a phone number, tell them the time and sometimes even inform them about the weather.

One day when Paul was small and his parents were out, he banged his thumb with a hammer. There was no point crying because there was nobody in. And then he remembered the telephone. Let Paul continue the story:

I got a stool, stood on it, and reached up to the handset: 'Information Please.'

The lady replied in her standard way, 'This is Information. How can I help you?'

'I've banged my thumb,' I sobbed.

'Is your mummy in?' Information Please asked.

'No.'

'Is your daddy in?'

'No.'

'Is it bleeding?'

'No.'

Information Please said, 'Can you get to the ice box?'

'Yes.'

'Hold some ice against it.'

It worked! After that I rang Information Please for everything. Information Please helped me with my geography homework – she told me where Philadelphia is. Information Please taught me how to spell *disappear*. And when my pet canary died and I cried down the phone and asked, 'Why would God make something that can sing so beautifully and let it die?' Information Please said, 'Paul, you must always remember there are other worlds to sing in.'

And then my parents moved to New York and I was out of her area, and anyway, I didn't believe that

Information Please could live in the new plastic phone. I never rang her again ... until I was twenty-four years old.

I was making a trip one day and my plane put down in the airport near where we used to live. I had about half an hour to wait and was sitting in the airport lounge when I saw a telephone. I thought, 'I wonder ...' I dialled and said, 'Information please' and a familiar voice said, 'This is Information.'

'Could you teach me to spell *disappear*?' I said.

There was a long pause and then she replied, 'I expect that thumb is better by now!'

I said, 'Have you any idea what you meant to me?'

She said, 'Have you any idea what you meant to *me*? We couldn't have children and I used to look forward to your calls. My name's Sally. I'm not very well and I only work a few hours a week, but if you're ever in the area, promise to ring me, won't you?'

After that, I rang Sally whenever I was in the area and we would talk. One day, I dialled the number and a different voice answered, 'This is Information.'

I said, 'Could I speak to Sally, please?'

'Are you a friend?' the woman said.

'Yes,' I replied, 'an old friend.'

There was a pause and the operator said, 'I'm so sorry to have to tell you, sir, but Sally died five weeks ago. She was elderly and hadn't been well for a long time.'

'Oh,' I said. 'I'm sorry to have troubled you.'

'No, wait,' the operator said. 'Is your name Paul?'

'Why, yes.'

'Well, sir, Sally said that if you happened to ring we must be sure to give you this message: "Paul, you must always remember there are other worlds to sing in."'[2]

Dianne and I got to know Roy and Fiona Castle in the few years before Roy died. He was one of the most versatile and popular entertainers of his generation, and many of you will remember him, perhaps particularly for presenting the TV show, Record Breakers. *When we spent time with Roy and Fiona, they would keep us enthralled with stories from their lives in show business. Roy told us of one occasion at the Royal Variety Performance when he and the comedian Tommy Cooper were standing in line before the show, waiting to be presented to the Queen.*

First of all, he said, when Tommy Cooper bowed to honour the Queen he almost nutted her, and then, when the Queen had passed Tommy and was about five people down the row, he turned and said in that unmistakable gruff voice, 'Excuse me, Your Majesty.'

The Queen turned to him, rather surprised: 'Yes?'

'Do you like football?'

The Queen looked totally bemused and replied, 'Not particularly.'

A big smile crossed Tommy's face as he said, 'Then is there any chance of having your Cup Final tickets?'

Roy's showbiz tales kept us entertained for hours, but the stories he told about his family life were the ones that touched me most.

A man looks back

DIANNE AND I were spending a night at Roy and Fiona's home. They have four children and we frequently spoke about family life. Chatting that evening before we went to bed, the mood turned thoughtful as Roy said suddenly, 'You know, in adult life at first there's just one pair of shoes in the hall, then if you get married there are two pairs of shoes. If children come along there are little pairs of shoes alongside yours, gradually those shoes get bigger, and one day they're not there any more. And then there are only two pairs of shoes again and finally . . . just one pair.'

We carried on talking and Roy told us that when he was a child, his father used to clean his shoes, and when his own children came along he decided to carry on that little tradition. During the night, I wrote a poem about it and read it to Roy and Fiona over breakfast. It seemed to touch Roy. A few weeks later, I went to the London Palladium in the West End to see him perform for the last time. Halfway through his set he sat on a stool and read the poem.

A Man Looks Back

I always cleaned the children's shoes –
the little (tiny!) patent shoes,
that covered feet fresh out of booties –
cleaned the black and made it shine,
removing final traces of stewed prune
and other culinary delights known only to the very young.

And as they grew, I cleaned a larger shoe.
Shoes that were strong enough to walk in almost!
Certainly strong enough for a toddler to take five steps . . .
and fall.

And then those first school shoes:
shoes that led such little feet
into a world full of such tomorrows.
And later, shoes, the toes of which
lost all their battles with footballs, gravel, and old tin cans;
new shoes that looked old within a week.

I cleaned them all.

And as each night I did the task,
a million memories came flooding back,
and I remembered a man long gone would clean our shoes,
six children in all,
my father cleaned each one,
as I now shine these for mine.

But children grow.
And shoes are for feet that move,
that take the boy into a man.
And I remember well the evening that I came
with cloth and brush as I had done so many times,
only to discover that, of course, the shoes had gone.

But they will come again, those shoes,
come again to me.
Oh, not for cleaning now –
other hands have long since done that task.
No, they will bring a man to me and a woman
holding the hands of tiny ones
with little feet.

And young eyes will look up and say,
'Grandpa, Mummy said . . . that you will clean my shoes.'

I was once invited to speak to some of the inmates at a prison. These men had read a book I'd written called The Sixty Minute Father, *and they'd been discussing some of the issues it raised in weekly parenting classes. As I stood before them that day, I can tell you quite honestly that I felt totally inadequate for the task.*

The red chair

WHEN I WALKED into the prison chapel where I was to speak to a group of the inmates, the looks on their faces and their body language clearly said: 'What do *you* know about being a father while in prison?'

My mind whirled. How could I enter into what these men were feeling? How could I understand anything about the special pressures on their families? Yet I desperately wanted to help them. I knew that they were suffering for the wrong they had done and yet, in addition to their personal regret, which was often very evident, their families too were paying a very high price. The opening lines of the talk I'd prepared seemed far too trite. And then, as I looked at them, a thought struck me:

'I know you do not choose to be in this institution,' I said. 'In fact, it's the last place you want to be – but you *have* chosen to be with me for this session on parenting. And, therefore, you have done today what many fathers don't do in the whole of a lifetime: you have taken some time to ask yourselves the simple question: "How can I be a better father?"'

I sensed the atmosphere change almost immediately. During the session, I told them about a businessman I had met who told me that he wasn't the emotional kind and couldn't bring himself to hug his children. I said that I'd suggested to him that he practise in front of a mirror!

At the end of our time together, one of the men approached me and said, 'The visiting room in the prison is cold and uninviting. When my family come to see me, we sit around a table. That table and the four chairs that surround it are screwed to the floor. One of the chairs is red and the prisoner has to sit on it. The room has a children's play area, but it's in the corner, and sometimes my child will call to me to join her playing there or she'll fall and need me. I get up to go to her and as I do, a warder will shout, "Hey, you! Get back on the red chair."'

The prisoner then said, 'Tell the man who can't bring himself to hug his kids about the man who can't get off the red chair.'

P.S. There is a good ending to this story. As I continued to speak to the prisoner, he said to me, 'Why don't you write a book about being a father in prison?'

I replied, 'Why don't you write one?'

'Nobody would ever publish it!' he answered.

I said, 'Care for the Family will publish it.'

Perhaps I didn't think he'd take me up on it – but he did. With the help of a wonderful family life teacher at the prison, he and others in his parenting class began to work with us to produce a book. It's called *Daddy's Working Away* (which is what mums in this situation often say to their children to explain their father's absence) and is a guide to being a dad in prison. You face some very special challenges in that situation. When you've got just fifty pence left on your telephone card, for instance, how on earth do you choose what to say to the son who's been waiting so patiently for his turn to speak to you, after all his brother and sisters. Do you do what his mother asked you and tell him off for whatever it is that he's just got himself into trouble over, or do you talk to him about his favourite football team and how you're both going to watch the game on *Match of the Day*?

Since that book was written, thousands of copies have been distributed in prisons all across the nation.

Parenting is a high calling. We are almost standing in the shoes of God and creating. I've heard the period when our children are small described as 'the special years' and I think that is a good definition. Those years are a special opportunity to build memories, to encourage, to develop character and impart values that may last a lifetime. But that window of opportunity passes so quickly. Somebody once said, 'The days are long, but the years are short.' I know of no clearer explanation of that than the song, 'Cat's in the Cradle'.[3]

Cat's in the cradle

My child arrived just the other day,
He came to the world in the usual way,
But there were planes to catch and bills to pay.
He learned to walk while I was away,
And he was talking 'fore I knew it, and as he grew,
He'd say, 'I'm gonna be like you, Dad,
You know I'm gonna be like you.'

And the cat's in the cradle and the silver spoon,
Little boy blue and the man in the moon.
'When you coming home, Dad?'
'I don't know when,
But we'll get together then, Son,
You know we'll have a good time then.'

My son turned ten just the other day,
He said, 'Thanks for the ball, Dad, come on let's play.
Can you teach me to throw?' I said, 'Not today,
I got a lot to do.' He said, 'That's OK.'
And he walked away, but his smile never dimmed,
Said, 'I'm gonna be like him, yeah.
You know I'm gonna be like him.'

And the cat's in the cradle and the silver spoon,
Little boy blue and the man in the moon.
'When you coming home, Dad?'
'I don't know when,
But we'll get together then, Son,
You know we'll have a good time then.'

Well, he came home from college just the other day,
So much like a man I just had to say,
'Son, I'm proud of you. Can you sit for a while?'
He shook his head, and he said with a smile,
'What I'd really like, Dad, is to borrow the car keys,
See you later,
Can I have them please?'

And the cat's in the cradle and the silver spoon,
Little boy blue and the man in the moon.
'When you coming home, Dad?'

'I don't know when,
But we'll get together then, Son,
You know we'll have a good time then.'

I've long since retired, and my son's moved away,
I called him up just the other day.
I said, 'I'd like to see you if you don't mind.'
He said, 'I'd love to, Dad, if I could find the time.
You see, my new job's a hassle, and the kids have the flu,
But it's sure nice talking to you, Dad.
It's been sure nice talking to you.'

And as I hung up the phone, it occurred to me,
He'd grown up just like me.
My boy was just like me.

And the cat's in the cradle and the silver spoon,
Little boy blue and the man in the moon.
'When you coming home, Son?'
'I don't know when,
But we'll get together then, Dad,
You know we'll have a good time then.'

There are few of us who won't feel guilty when we consider these issues, but the good news is that whatever their
age – whether they are three or thirty-three – we can make

a difference in our children's lives. Many a child has discovered a relationship with their mother or father years after leaving home, but even at that stage of life, the same two ingredients are needed as when our children are small: time, and the courage to seize the day.

Having said that, there is no doubt that the time we spend with our children in the early years is vital – they are indeed 'the special years'. So consider the eighteen years of childhood and imagine for a moment that an egg-timer contained not sand but days. When your child was born, there were 6,570 days in it. If your child is ten years old, 3,650 have already gone. You have 2,920 left. No amount of money, power or prestige can increase that number. Don't miss one of them.

When I met with some trusted friends over thirty years ago to discuss starting a new charity, one of them said, 'You and Dianne will be able to tour the country telling people how to build strong marriages.'

'Ah,' I replied, 'there's a bit of a problem with that.'

'What kind of problem?'

'Well,' I said, 'we've been married for over fifteen years, but we've been through some very tough times – times when we didn't feel much in love.'

My friend answered in a heartbeat. 'All right,' he said. 'Then tell people about that.' And so one of the foundation blocks of Care for the Family was laid: vulnerability.

Fellow travellers

VULNERABILITY IS IMPORTANT when working with families; it says to them, 'We are fellow travellers. We've made the same mistakes that you've made – and we can find answers together.' When I talk to people who are considering volunteering for Care for the Family, I say something like this:

We are so grateful for your willingness to consider working with us, but there is a little caveat: if you have the perfect marriage, have never had a row, spend most evenings gazing into each other's eyes and you can't wait to share your pearls of wisdom with struggling couples . . . you probably aren't our kind of person. And if your children do the washing-up every night, save up their pocket money for study guides, keep an immaculately tidy bedroom and you've got a blog called 'Steps to Perfect Parenting' to help less able parents . . . you, too, are probably not the kind of volunteer we're looking for. The people we need to work with us are those who have cried a little – or who can, at least, *imagine* tough times hitting their *own* home.

Vulnerability is important because it whispers to us, 'You are not alone – others have walked this path before you.' And vulnerability not only enables us to encourage others by allowing them to identify with us, but it helps us to empathise with others as we share our experiences.

I remember meeting with one of our Bereaved Parent Support team who had just run a residential weekend for bereaved parents. Those gathered may have lost a child through different circumstances – illness, accident or even murder – and all were grieving that life could never be the same again. I asked Peter, the leader, how the weekend had gone. 'Well, Rob,' he said, 'on the Friday afternoon when the parents first arrived, some of them – especially the men – sat with their arms folded as if to say, "We shouldn't have come. You can't give us back our child." And then I told them how we lost our son when he was twenty-one. I told them that my wife and I love each other, but she couldn't get near me. I would just walk and cry. I didn't want to take my life, but I didn't want to live either. Sometimes people would say to me, "Peter, time will heal." But it doesn't heal. I now understand that it's not meant to heal. The pain gets easier, but it never heals. And once in a while someone would say, "But, Peter, you've still got three other great kids." And I'd reply, "I know. But I want *him*."'

And then he said, 'I saw the incredible effect of sharing our stories and our pain with these parents. By Sunday afternoon it was as if they had opened up like flowers in the sun. It's not that we'd given them easy answers – there *are* no easy answers. It was just that we'd given them the understanding that others have walked, and are walking, this way and they are coming through it – there is hope.'

One father who, on the Friday, had obviously found the whole experience very difficult, came up to Peter just as they left on Sunday and whispered simply, 'Thank you.'

That's why we believe in vulnerability.

In the work I do, I see enough pain in a week to last me a lifetime. I know there's not a family in the world that can avoid the tough times. But I also know that family life is stronger, more able to withstand challenges and difficulties, if there is a bank of laughter it can draw on. As I look back over my own family life, there's one story that, for me, sums all this up. I have told it all over the world. Sometimes people ask me, 'Is it really true?' I am afraid it is – every word.

Let's go fishing

WE WERE ON a family holiday and near where we were staying there was a big lake where people were fishing. Suddenly my son Lloyd said, 'Dad, can we go fishing?'

'We haven't got a rod, Son,' I replied, but he was fourteen and he was not to be stopped. He found a long twig and tied a piece of string on to make a line, then he put a safety pin on to act as a hook and attached a big lump of bread from one of his sandwiches to the end of it.

Never in the history of the world have fish been in so little danger. They examined the bread, picked bits off at will, and shared it out among their friends and neighbours.

Despite this, I was getting quite engrossed in our little effort and that's when it happened: I heard a loud noise from further along the bank. I turned and saw a group of fishermen. They had expensive rods and every conceivable fishing aid . . . and they were laughing at us. Now, I'm not proud of what happened next, but I threw our makeshift rod to the ground and stalked off across the road. I made my way to a restaurant, where I'd seen fish displayed outside for sale earlier that day (dead ones, that is). I bought one; it cost me almost five pounds.

I rushed back to the lake and as surreptitiously as possible secured the fish to the safety pin on the end of our rod and lowered the line into the lake. I said, 'Lloyd, when some people come past, I want you to yell out as loud as you can, "Dad, I think you've got one!"' He gave me a sympathetic look, but said, 'OK, I'll do it.'

After about five minutes, a group of people came towards us along the little path that skirted the lake. When they drew near, Lloyd yelled out, 'Dad, I think you've got one!' The people turned to look and, to my delight, so did the fishermen who had been laughing at us. I pulled on the twig and yanked the string from the water. The fish was fixed firmly to the end, its scales glinting in the afternoon sun – a fine specimen indeed.

I turned to the crowd to enjoy my moment, but instead of looks of admiration, there were signs of acute embarrassment. People started talking among themselves and sidled off along the path. The fishermen further along were sniggering. I didn't understand. 'What went wrong, Lloyd?'

He was helpless with laughter. In fact, he was rolling on the grass, holding his sides. It took several minutes before he could say anything, but finally he spluttered it out: 'Two things, Dad. First, you should have jiggled the line a bit – it looked dead!' He paused and started laughing again. 'And second, you put the hook – through its tail.'

When I'm gone I want my children to look back and say, 'He put values into our lives, he taught us to care for those who have less than we have, he urged us to keep the faith.' But I think I'd somehow have missed it if they didn't also say, 'Wasn't the old boy crazy at times? Do you remember some of the stuff he had us doing?'

Somebody once said to me, 'You've written lots of books; if you could just pick a couple of lines from any one of them, what would they be?' I was able to answer in a heartbeat. The words are from *The Sixty Minute Father*:

'When they were little you used to tickle them. Don't ever stop.'

The world is full of people who want us to be just like them. They could be friends, employers or even parents. Instead of helping us to discover our personal talents and strengths, they try to make us into someone that we just can't be. I often meet people who are near the end of their life yet have never had anybody to help them discover their incredible uniqueness — the one thing that they can do best.

Let the rabbits run

IMAGINE THERE IS a meadow. In that meadow is a duck, a fish, an eagle, a squirrel and a rabbit. They decide they want to have a school for their children so they can be clever, just like people. They come up with a curriculum they believe will make for a well-rounded animal: running, swimming, tree-climbing, jumping and . . . flying.

On his first day of school, little Bertie Rabbit combed his ears and went off to his running class. There, he was a star. He ran to the top of the hill and back as fast as he could go, and oh, didn't it feel good!

The next class was swimming. When the rabbit sniffed the water he said, 'Wait a minute! Rabbits don't like to swim.'

The instructor said, 'Well, you may not like it, but five years from now you'll know it was a good thing for you to learn to do.'

In the tree-climbing lesson, a tree trunk was set at a thirty-degree angle so all the animals had a chance to succeed. Bertie tried so hard that he hurt his leg. In the jumping lesson, he got along well. In the flying lesson, he had a real problem, so the teacher gave him a psychological test and discovered he belonged in remedial flying.

The next morning he went to his swimming lesson. The instructor said, 'Today we jump into the water.'

'Wait, wait! I talked to my parents about swimming. They didn't learn to swim. We don't like to get wet. I'd like to drop this class.'

The instructor said, 'You can't drop it now. At this point you have a choice: either you jump in or you fail.'

Bertie jumped in. He panicked! He went down once. He went down twice. Bubbles came up. The instructor saw that he was drowning and pulled him out. The other animals had never seen anything quite as funny as this wet rabbit who looked more like a rat, and so they chirped and jumped and barked and laughed at the rabbit. The little rabbit was more humiliated than he had ever been in his life. He wanted desperately to get away from the lesson that day. He was glad when it was over and headed for home – at least his mum and dad would understand

and help him. When he arrived, he told them, 'I don't like school. I just want to be free.'

'If rabbits are going to get ahead in this world, you have to get your diploma,' replied his parents.

'I don't want a diploma,' Bertie said.

'You're going to get a diploma whether you like it or not,' his parents replied.

They argued and finally the parents made Bertie go to bed. In the morning, he headed off to school with a slow hop. Then he remembered that the head teacher had said that any time he had a problem, the school counsellor's door was always open. When he arrived at school, he hopped up in the chair by the school counsellor and said, 'I don't like school.'

The school counsellor said, 'Mmmm – tell me about it.' And he did.

The school counsellor said, 'Rabbit, I hear you. I hear you say that you don't like school because you don't like swimming. I think I have diagnosed that correctly. I'll tell you what we'll do. You're doing well in running, so I don't know why you need to work on that. I'll arrange it so you don't have to go running any more. You can have two periods of swimming instead.' When Bertie heard that, he was very upset!

As he hopped out of the school counsellor's office, he looked up and saw his friend the wise old owl, who cocked his head and said, 'Rabbit, life doesn't have to be this way. We could have schools and businesses where people are allowed to concentrate on what they do well.'

Bertie Rabbit was inspired. He thought that when he graduated, he would start a business where the rabbits would do nothing but run, the squirrels could just climb trees, and the fish could swim all day long. As he disappeared into the meadow, he sighed softly to himself and said, 'Oh, my, what a great place that would be.'[4]

I've had the opportunity of talking with thousands of individuals about their childhood, and time and again those who spoke of strong families also spoke of traditions. Whether these families were rich or poor, lived in the country or the inner city, were headed by a mother and father or a single parent, their response was the same. When I asked them to tell me what made the memories of their family life sweet, they'd start the sentence, 'We always . . .'

We always . . .

THE TRADITIONS PEOPLE have shared with me have been many and varied. They are often to do with special days of the year. One family said they always light candles on Christmas Eve and watch *It's a Wonderful Life*. Another family always go for a walk in a busy park on Boxing Day and as people come towards them, they try to guess what presents they are wearing! One family sing 'Auld Lang Syne' holding hands together in the street outside their home on New Year's Eve, and then have a curry afterwards, sharing hopes and dreams for the year ahead around the table.

Of course, sometimes those telling me their stories realised that the memories they were sharing were simple – even a little embarrassing. But once they got the confidence to talk to me, then no matter how old they were, the traditions came tumbling out. One very sophisticated lawyer remembered having the following conversation with her father every evening when she was small:

'Daddy, can I sit on your lap?'
'No. Only little girls with brown eyes can sit on my lap.'
'I've got brown eyes!'
'Well, only little girls with brown eyes and black hair can sit on my lap.'
'Daddy, I've got brown eyes and black hair!'
'Well, only little girls with brown eyes, black hair and pink shoes can sit on my lap . . .'

And, finally, a small child with brown eyes, black hair, pink shoes and, some nights, a dozen other carefully chosen attributes, would climb onto her father's knee. And when she was old, she still remembered it.

It's no secret that one of my richest sources of stories is my children. So rich is this vein that during times of writer's block, I have sometimes wished we'd had more of them!

A little education from a dog

WHEN MY SON Lloyd was fourteen, he asked me if he could have a dog. I wasn't sure this was a good idea. We'd never had one before and all of my friends' dogs seemed to be slightly mad, but somebody told me a dog is good for a boy. Perhaps they were right. Lloyd assured me that if we bought him a dog he would be devoted to the creature. In fact, he would spend so much time walking it and generally seeing to its welfare that he wouldn't have time to go out with his mates or spend hours on the phone.

We bought him a dog.

When he was nineteen, I told him the dog was still alive.

But perhaps it wasn't all lost on Lloyd. Robert Benchley

said, 'A boy can learn a lot from a dog: obedience, loyalty, and the importance of turning around three times before lying down.' Here are some other things you can learn from a dog.

1. When loved ones come home, always run to greet them.
2. When it's in your best interest, practise obedience.
3. Let others know when they've invaded your territory.
4. Run, romp and play daily.
5. Be loyal.
6. Never pretend to be something you're not.
7. If what you want lies buried, dig until you find it.
8. When someone is having a bad day, sit close by and nuzzle them gently.
9. Thrive on attention.
10. Avoid biting when a simple growl will do.
11. When you're happy, dance around and wag your entire body.
12. No matter how often you're scolded, don't buy into the guilt thing and pout . . . run right back and make friends.
13. Delight in the simple joy of a long walk.

Jezz turned out to be the epitome of all that we had hated in other people's dogs. He barked a lot, he jumped up on you when you came in, and he cocked his leg against anything that stayed still for over five seconds (a compelling incentive for houseguests to keep on the move).

On one occasion when Dianne was having a particularly hassling day and while she was in the middle of a phone conversation with a woman who was sharing some deeply traumatic experience, one of the kids came into the kitchen and said, 'Mum, Jezz has just fallen through the lounge ceiling.' And so he had. Somebody had left the door of a small cupboard open on a half landing, Jezz had decided to look inside, trod on an unboarded area and, hey presto: one collie cowering in the corner of the room and a dog-shaped hole in the ceiling.

When I was leaving for a trip to Africa once, I was about to get in the taxi that was parked outside my home when I suddenly asked the driver to wait a moment. I rushed back into the house and looked for Jezz. I found him lolling in the corner of a room – he hadn't been well for a week. I rubbed his head and said, 'See you, Jezz.'

By the time I got back, he had died. I don't expect everybody to understand this, but it affected me deeply. I felt I could still hear him . . . see him, even. I cried a lot.

I was grateful I'd taken a little time just before I left to show him I cared. But I was grateful for more than that because there are people in my life I love a whole lot more than Jezz, and it was a reminder that I would be wise not to take them for granted. It's not enough to love; we have to take time to show we love – to demonstrate it.

It's just one more thing I learnt from a dog.

One evening, during an event at the Birmingham Symphony Hall, I sat on a stool and read aloud an incredible children's story by Max Lucado called You Are Special. *The story is about Punchinello, a wooden Wemmick who is despised by all the other Wemmicks and seems to hate himself. One day, everything changes when he meets Eli, the old carpenter who made him. Eli convinces him that he is unique, loved and special.*

As I finished reading the story, I heard a woman crying somewhere in the middle of the two-thousand-strong audience. But rather than a cry of despair, it seemed to me to be one of relief. Perhaps she understood at last that she was loved for who she was. She could leave the mask behind.

Bring on the clowns

WHEN I WAS five years old, my father took three
friends and me to the circus. I really can't remember
what impressed the others, but I fell in love with the
clowns. The reason for such high emotion in a small boy
is not hard to figure out: they juggled without dropping,
fell without hurting, and had a total disregard for authority.
For all those reasons, they were my heroes. But compelling
as such qualities were, they weren't the main reason they
captivated me. No, I fell in love with the clowns because
they were never sad.

I can't quite remember why that was so important to
me at such a tender age. I suppose it's because in my sixty
months or so on this planet I had known some trauma.
There was the day my rabbit died, and the time the head

came off my favourite soldier. Even now I can taste the salt of the tears those events brought. But the clowns always laughed; no sorrow touched them – they were immune.

And I loved them for that reason until I was nine. Two days after my ninth birthday, I watched a film on television about a circus. As I sat there, glued to the screen, the camera suddenly moved away from the ring to a nearby caravan. Written on the door in fancy lettering were the words, 'The home of Coco'. By the wonders of technology, I was taken inside the inner sanctuary of the greatest clown who had ever lived. My hero sat on a bed, tears ran down his face, and by his side lay a mask that smiled up at him. I cried too, but I wasn't sure why.

Many years later I wrote a poem about that incident. Perhaps I understood at last why it had made me cry.

The Mask of a Clown

I have played the part so long,
Worn the make-up and the smile,
Took the bow and the applause,
Said, 'Oh fine, oh, yes, of course . . . I'm fine.'

Donned the costume, trod the boards,
Learnt the lines and sung the song,
Made you laugh and made you cry.
I have done it all so long.

I have done it all so long,
That I don't expect you see,
That to get this leading role,
The real cost was . . . me.

Quite recently, I came across another clown story. It touched me deeply.

A man went to the doctor's one day. He described various ailments, but the GP perceived that underneath it all was a deep sadness. At the end of the interview, the doctor said, 'I think I can help you.' Opening his desk drawer, he reached in and took out two tickets to a circus that was coming to town; they were a gift from a grateful patient, but he knew he would never use them. The doctor said, 'Grimaldi, the great clown, is appearing. Go and watch him; he'll make you laugh.'

The patient graciously took the tickets, but just as he was leaving he turned and said, 'Sir, I am Grimaldi.'

One night I gave a closing address at a Christian conference. I had spoken on the fact that God knows the worst about us and yet loves us unconditionally – that he is our Father. I suppose I spoke for thirty minutes or so, but when I had finished, the man who had been chairing the event made his way towards the microphone and told a simple story. It took him no more than a couple of minutes, but as soon as he finished it, I knew that if he'd told it at the beginning, I need never have spoken. Here is the event Jeff Lucas spoke of that night, as told in his book, Walking Backwards.

Loved

I picked up the phone and my fears were confirmed: Dad was dying. I was to cancel everything and rush home immediately on the next plane . . . Two hours later, I rushed into Dad's hospital room. He was conscious and as I took his hand and smoothed his hair, he smiled but said nothing. My dad had been unable to speak for some four years. He loved to talk but that gift had been taken from him by a stroke that reduced his speech to meaningless drivel.

Now, as I sat at his bedside, I knew that time was short. 'Dad, I love you so very much. You know that, don't you?' He smiled, but then his eyes clouded over. I could see he was struggling to say something important, but the words wouldn't come out. However, he had overcome this handicap before. My dad knew how to communicate without words.

Some months earlier I'd been staying overnight at my parents' home. It was the end of the day, and I had already retired to my room. There was a knock on the door. Dad came in and knelt down silently by the bed. He took the blankets and the sheets and tucked me in, just like he'd done thirty-five years earlier when I was his five-year-old. With a kiss on my cheek, brushing away a stray hair on my face, he was gone. I lay there in the dark, aware that here was I, a forty-year-old adult, so used to making decisions and fending for my family and myself, and I had just been tucked in and made warm and secure by my frail father. It felt good.

Jeff then looked out at four thousand people and said, 'God wants to tuck some of you in tonight – to let you know again that you are loved.' As he spoke, I watched the audience. I could both see and feel emotion bursting out all over the arena. Grown men and women were realising, some of them for the first time in their lives, an incredible truth.

You are loved.

Dianne and I have been married for over forty years. You can't be married that long without going through tough times, and we have certainly experienced those — times, even, when I think we both wondered if we would ever make it through together. About twenty years into our marriage, I wrote the following poem. I think I can say that I would write the same words today.

To my wife

I Have Loved You

I have loved you.
Loved you when we held hands feverishly,
in the back of the Gaumont cinema in Queen Street.

And I have loved you.
Loved you when we were married.
Loved you as we scoured junk shops, furnishing our first flat
and picking up fantastic bargains
(and wardrobes with woodworm in them!).

We built a home.
And I loved you when she was born,

and suddenly we were three.
And then he came, and throughout all the sunshine and the joy,
I have loved you.

And I have loved you in the darkness, when we cried together,
and the tunnel seemed so very long and so very black.
And you loved me, with all the inconsistency and hypocrisy,
when all great hopes came so often to so little,
went on loving.

And we have loved each other, you and I.
Loved when at times it seemed that love had died,
and all there was, was just the hope that it would grow again –
come fighting, kicking through the frost.
And it did, came stronger, purer, finer, truer.

And today it is Saturday, and today I can say,
I have loved you.

Every year, we receive thousands of pieces of communication, yet the particular letter I am about to share with you has become iconic in the life of Care for the Family.

The letter

THE MARRIAGE EVENT this story refers to was one of the very first that Dianne and I spoke at, held on a Saturday to help couples strengthen – or even save – their marriage. Shortly after the event, we received a letter:

Dear Rob and Dianne,

On Saturday, my husband and I attended the 'Marriage Matters' seminar. It was a day that changed our lives. In the morning, before leaving our home, I said to my husband, 'I think this seminar is our last hope; if nothing good comes of it, I think we may have to part.'

You see, after fourteen years of marriage, he'd had an affair. I've not been able to forgive him.

However sorry he said he was, I simply could not. That was, until Saturday. But when you spoke about the possibility of forgiveness, I thought, how can I not forgive?

And your words made me think so much about my children, my little girl and my little boy: they deserve a happy life, a mother and a father to love and to care for them. The whole day made us look at our family; we talked so much that night, and we're still talking. We laughed a lot, and at the end of the day we cried together. Thank you. Saturday changed our lives.

P.S. Here's to the next fourteen years!

How hard it must have been for her to write that letter. And I knew that however sincerely she believed what she'd written, the road ahead to working out that forgiveness would be long and hard. As I think about that, it reminds me of another young couple who'd attended one of our marriage events. They waited until the auditorium was empty and then approached me. He spoke first. He said, 'We've been married for a few years but some months ago I had an affair – a one-night stand. I was so sorry afterwards and I begged my wife to forgive me. I wanted her to know how much I meant it when I said that it would never happen again, so one night I took my wedding ring off, gave it to her, and said, "Don't put that back on my finger until you're sure you can trust me again."'

And then he showed me a ring on his third finger and said, 'Last week she put it back on my hand.' He looked happy, but as I turned to his wife, her head was bowed. I thought for a moment and said, 'Forgive me if I'm wrong, but I think that when your wife put that ring back on your hand she was not saying, "I trust you again." She was actually saying, "With all my heart I *want* to trust you again."' She lifted her head and said, 'That's exactly how I feel.'

I have often thought about the woman who wrote the letter above. I know that forgiveness like that is not always possible, but *she* decided to give it. Forgiveness is not magic. When we try to forgive it does not mean that the memories or the hurts will go, that we won't occasionally still wake up with that sick feeling in our stomachs, or that we won't still have to look away when we pass a place that brings back painful recollections. But for that couple, forgiveness gave them a chance: it was the key that allowed them to at least try again.

Ten years after she first wrote, the woman sent another letter with a photograph. It was of her, her husband, and their two teenage children smiling out at the camera. I turned the Polaroid over and over in my hand and wondered at the story that lay behind it, and whether the children knew, or would ever know, about what had nearly torn their home apart. And I thought of a woman's resolve and the sheer courage it often takes to even begin *to forgive*. I got all our staff together, showed them the photograph and said, 'This is why we do what we do. I know it's not possible for every family to stay together, but I want you to know that I would have done it all – all the writing, all the speaking, all the travelling – just to see these two kids with their parents. For me, from now on, everything else is a bonus.'

The first letter came almost thirty years ago, the second with the photograph of the children twenty years ago, and recently we received another one from the same woman: it contained an invitation to their fortieth wedding celebration.

One of the hardest things about parenting is that most of the time you don't really know how you are doing. One minute you're feeling quietly confident or even quite proud of yourself (Supermum or Superdad personified) and the next you are convinced that you're the worst mother or father who ever lived.

'Everybody Else's Father'

WHEN MY SON Lloyd was a teenager, I remember asking him a question about something that was puzzling me. Although I was sure it wasn't a big deal, it was eating away at me and I thought it best we sorted it out. It's just that on the very day he hit eleven, another person emerged in our relationship. I call him 'Everybody Else's Father'. I said to Lloyd, 'Who is this guy?'

I first came across him when Lloyd wanted to sleep over at Billy's house. I had never heard of Billy and, frankly, there was precious little information coming from Lloyd. For all I knew, a sleepover at Billy's could have been in the same category as a night on the town in Beirut. I said, 'No.' And it was then that the character who was, in future, to make regular appearances in our lives, stepped out of the shadows. Lloyd burst into tears and said, 'Everybody Else's Father is letting them go.'

He slept over at Billy's.

Since that fateful day, this mystery man poked his nose into just about every conflict Lloyd and I have ever had. 'Everybody Else's Father' let his child go to a disco the evening before the GCSE maths exam. 'Everybody Else's Father' let his offspring have his ear, nose and belly button pierced. And 'Everybody Else's Father' gave his kids amounts of pocket money that made me look like I needed a visit from Marley's ghost.

The strange thing is that although I thought I had met the parents of all of my son's friends, I had still not come across this man in the flesh. In fact, so far as I can tell, all the other parents were just about as scared, stingy and boring as me.

So I offered to strike a deal with Lloyd. The next time he resorted to using this character, I said I'd agree to whatever he wanted so long as he produce the man. I mean real, live 'Everybody Else's Father' in my living room. Even if that meant I had to agree to Lloyd doing a bungee jump off the Eiffel Tower, it would be worth it.

And once I'd met 'Everybody Else's Father', I knew exactly what I would do: I'd ring every parent I'd ever met and tell them I'd caught the guy, he was locked in my garage, and dying to meet us all . . .

Maybe you will find it hard to believe, but I can honestly say that, with one or two exceptions (when it seemed as though I was pushing a large blancmange up a hill), no matter how often I tell a story I am still touched by it. It's certainly not a case of going through the motions; sometimes the tears will start rolling down my face even though I've related it hundreds of times before. I feel sure that this next story will continue to move me even if I go on telling it until I'm a hundred!

The day her father left

LISTEN TO THIS woman's memory of an event that happened when she was a child. She remembers word for word a conversation that took place with her father in the hallway of her home.

'Darling,' he said, 'I know it's been bad for you these past few days, and I don't want to make it worse, but there's something I have to tell you. Your mum and I are getting a divorce.'

'But Daddy!'

'I know you don't want this, but it has to be done. Your mum and I don't get along like we used to. I've already packed. In fact, I have to catch a plane that's leaving shortly.'

'But Daddy, why do you have to leave?'

'Well, darling, your mum and I can't live together any longer.'

'I know that, but why do you have to leave our town?'

'Well, I've got somebody else waiting for me now.'

'Daddy, will I see you again?'

'Of course you will, darling, we'll work something out.'

'But what? You'll be living away and I'll be here!'

'Maybe your mum will agree to your spending a few weeks with me in the summer and perhaps two in the winter.'

'Why not more often?'

'I don't think she'll agree even to that, darling, much less more.'

'Daddy, it can't hurt to try.'

'I know, but we'll have to work it out later. Now look, my plane leaves soon and I must get to the airport. I'm going to get my luggage. I want you to go to your room so you don't have to watch me go – and no long goodbyes, either.'

'OK, Daddy, goodbye. Don't forget to write to me.'

'I won't. Goodbye. Now, go on upstairs.'

'Daddy, I don't want you to go!'

'I know, but I have to.'

'Why?'

'You wouldn't understand.'

'Yes, I would.'

'No, you wouldn't.'

'Oh – well, goodbye.'

'Goodbye. Now go to your room. Hurry up, now.'

And then she remembered saying, 'OK, Daddy, I guess that's the way life goes sometimes.'

Her father replied, 'Yes, darling, that's the way life goes sometimes.'

After her father walked out the door, she never saw him again.

Some years ago, I said to Dianne, 'There are times when I think I'd like to get out of the rat race.' In reply, my wife smiled sweetly, 'The problem with that, darling, is that you love it. At heart, you're a rat!'

Just too busy

DO YOU HATE stopping for petrol? If so, it could be because when you pull into the service station you see all the cars you'd previously overtaken going past!

Do you do most things quickly? Walking, talking and eating? People say, 'You're such a fast eater!' (What they really mean is, 'Am I so boring to talk to that you've finished your main course while I'm still on my starter?')

When you are driving, do you swap lanes in traffic jams even though you know full well about the eternal law that says the lane you have just joined will now move more slowly than the lane you have just left? As you are hurtling down the motorway, do you catch yourself doing complicated mathematical sums: 'Manchester is 90 miles away. If I drive at 90 it'll take me an hour. If I drive at 180 it would take me half an hour. If I drive at 70 . . . No, that's too difficult'?

These characteristics are typical of a personality profile that psychologists call Type A. The theory about this behaviour type began with two cardiologists, Friedman and Rosenman, noticing that some of the patients with heart conditions were unable to sit in their seats in the waiting room for long. They tended to sit on the edge of the seat and leap up frequently, and they wore out the chairs in a particular way. Typically, the back areas of a chair are worn down, but what was unusual was that these people wore out the front edges and the armrests. They were like racehorses ready to burst out of the gate.

Even if we want to take issue with Friedman and Rosenman's findings, many of us recognise the personality type. Of course, Type A people often achieve a lot, but sometimes the price is very high – not only emotionally, but physically. In fact, in several studies, this type of behaviour has been shown to be a significant contributor to the development of coronary heart disease.

Some psychologists have suggested that underlying this lifestyle is a need to prove ourselves. Perhaps that's what the writer of the book of Ecclesiastes was hinting at when he said: 'I saw that all toil and all achievement spring from one person's envy of another.'[5] Those of us caught on this treadmill have no resting place, for we must always move on to the next thing. We even feel guilty when we try to relax; holidays are often not an oasis but something to be endured until we can get back to the security of activity.

And there is an even greater problem with regard to our spiritual lives: we have the ability to run on empty long after the reality of faith in our heart and any real sense of communion with God has gone.

Nobody sums up both the dilemma and the solution for me as well as Henri Nouwen:

> I realised that I was caught in a web of strange paradoxes. While complaining about too many demands, I felt uneasy when none were made. While speaking about the burden of letter writing, an empty mailbox made me sad. While fretting about tiring lecture tours, I felt disappointed when there were no invitations. While speaking nostalgically about an empty desk, I feared the day on which that would come true. In short, while desiring to be alone, I was frightened of being left alone. The more I became aware of these paradoxes, the more I started to see how much I had indeed fallen in love with my own compulsions and illusions, and how much I needed to step back and wonder, 'Is there a quiet stream underneath the fluctuating

affirmations and rejections of my little world? Is
there a still point where my life is anchored and
from which I can reach out with hope and courage
and confidence?"[6]

May we each grasp the freedom of having nothing to
prove.

When I wrote The Money Secret *I was searching for a way to explain the foolishness of buying things on credit just to keep up with the Joneses. After crunching up pages and pages of failed efforts and hurling them in the waste bin, I wrote the following piece.*

The alien and the earthling

AN ALIEN AND an earthling were hovering above the M25 motorway and watching the passing cars. The alien was trying to understand how dwellers of the tiny planet conducted their affairs. 'What are these two cars directly beneath us?' he asked.

'One is called a Ferrari and the other is a Mondeo,' replied the earthling.

'I can see that one is very cramped – in fact, the child in the back seat looks as if he is dying for lack of air – but the one you call a Mondeo has four large seats and lots of room. It's easy to see that the Ferrari must be for your poorer people.'

The earthling laughed out loud. 'No – the Ferrari is seven times as expensive as the Mondeo!'

The alien looked puzzled. 'That must be because the running costs are much less expensive.'

The earthling was beside himself at the alien's naivety. 'No – they're four times greater than the Mondeo.'

'Will it hold its value better than the Mondeo?'

'No, it will drop in value in the first year to a sum equal to the total cost of the Mondeo!'

'How do most people pay for the Ferrari?'

'They go to a moneylender – we call them finance companies – and they pay the moneylender interest every month.'

'So they are not wealthy people?'

'Well, they're not short of a bob or two, but no, most of them don't have enough cash to buy a Ferrari.'

'Why would anybody who can't really afford it pay all that interest to have the cramped car when they could have the one with all the room in it?'

The earthling was enjoying explaining things to his slower visitor. 'For two reasons: first, the Ferrari does almost 200 miles an hour!'

Even the alien was impressed – that was equal to one of their smaller intergalactic run-abouts. 'Wow! Does the driver ever go that fast in it?'

'Oh no, by law he can only go seventy miles an hour – the same as the Mondeo driver. If he kept breaking the speed limit, he'd be put in prison!'

The alien was totally confused but eager to learn. 'You said there were two reasons.'

'Well, the second is that only very successful people can afford to own the Ferrari; when you drive one of these, other people know that you are clever.'

It was the alien's turn to smile. 'Now I can see why humans have been desperate to try and find intelligent life on other planets.'

I often tell a story about a man called Arthur. He died a few years ago but just before he did, I wrote an article about him. I'd like to share it with you now.

The man who changed my life

THE MAN WHO changed my life is dying.

Arthur is almost eighty now. I visit him at the hospital – he is practically comatose. I sit by his bed and allow my mind to drift back over the years.

I remember meeting Arthur as I walked down a street near my home. I was in my mid-teens and life was not exactly humming. School seemed like a foreign country from which I was about to be deported. My teacher had written in my report, 'He is making no use of what little ability he has.' My parents didn't go to church but I'd gone to the Sunday school at the end of our road since I was small, although I was about to drop out of that. My twin ambitions were to become a rock and roll singer and to snog Carol Pearce (I achieved one of them – and that only briefly).

When we met that day in the street, Arthur told me that he was starting a Bible course in his home and asked if I'd like to come. If your main dream is to perform at sell-out concerts and have girls throw articles of clothing at you, a Bible study on a Wednesday night might not seem like the greatest offer you've ever had. But for some reason I said yes.

In some ways Arthur had little going for him in the home study arena. First, he had never passed an academic examination and he had little grasp of theology. Second, Arthur had a speech impediment; he often got his words horribly mangled. And the home where we had the study wasn't exactly palatial; Arthur and his wife Margaret were poor – they had just two small rooms in his mother's house. But they had something that made up for all of this: they loved kids – especially ones who didn't fit in to church too easily. They loved us by not boring us for longer than twenty-five minutes with the Bible study and by using some of the little money they had to buy us fish and chips afterwards. And they loved us by setting up a table tennis table made out of two bits of hardboard. (There was only a foot of space at either end – if the ball went under the table we had to perform an engineering job to retrieve it.) And they loved us by hunting us down if we ever missed a week. But most of all, they made us feel special. No matter what teachers said about you, when you walked into Arthur's home, you felt like a king.

When I was seventeen, Arthur told me that he thought God had given me a gift of public speaking. I told him to forget it – I wasn't the kind of kid even to put my hand up in class. Arthur said I didn't have a choice in the matter: if God had given me a gift, then I was stuck with it, and he was going to help me develop it. This was not an encouraging prospect – Arthur wasn't the most skilled orator you'd ever meet.

But teach me he did, and he made me practise in his 'best room' with my notes perched on the mantelpiece. And one day he told me I was ready to face my public: at first talking to children and later to adults.

In the years since then I have spoken to many people across the world. On one occasion, I had been invited to address a conference attended by more than a thousand lawyers in Vienna. Just before it started, I called Arthur and said, 'I'm about to go on stage. You taught me to do this. Thank you.' He said, 'Did I?'

A few years after that, I was being interviewed about one of my books on a radio station in America. During the programme, they rang Arthur at his home as a surprise to me. The three of us talked for a while and, at the end, the presenter asked him what he now thought of the boy who used to come to his Bible class. He said, 'I'm proud of him.' I cried on air.

So I sit by his hospital bed and watch him. He taught me so much. He taught me that you don't have to be young to be a great youth worker, and you don't have to have great talent to be used by God; you just have to be prepared to use what you do have. And he taught me that if you can't do something yourself, you can still help somebody else do it – and so touch the lives of people you may never see. But above all, Arthur and Margaret taught me that the greatest gift really is love.

Now it is time for me to leave the hospital. I bend over him and kiss his forehead. And then I turn back and put my mouth close to his ear. I whisper, 'Thank you. You changed my life.'

My mother-in-law, Anne, had Alzheimer's disease during the last few years of her life. It was a difficult time for her and for those of us who loved her so much, but as well as the deep sadness, there were also times of joy. I wrote this piece just a few months before she died.

Beyond the grip of Alzheimer's

WHEN I VISIT Dianne's mother with her, I watch the interaction between a mother and her daughter. As soon as Dianne enters the room, this old lady's face lights up. Such recognition used to prompt Dianne to say, 'Do you remember my name?' But too many disappointments have stopped her asking that question. Instead, Dianne will say, 'You look pretty today' or 'You've got your new cardigan on!' And again her mother will smile with no less pleasure than she did when, as a young bride, her husband, long since dead now, whispered in the church, 'You look lovely!'

Then there will be some minutes when Anne just talks. It is true there will be moments of clarity, but for the most part, it will be a jumble of gentle nonsense until Dianne interrupts and says, 'What shall we do today?' In truth, Anne will never leave her bed again, but one advantage of her confused mind is that almost anything is possible. And soon a mother and her daughter are planning a shopping trip.

'Shall we take the bus or go by car?' asks Dianne.

'Oh!' shrieks Anne, 'the bus!'

'And what do we need to get?' says Dianne, reaching for a pen and paper. I smile as I watch an old lady, who once ran a large office, dictate a list so fast that Dianne (now her junior secretary!) can hardly keep up. But there is never a demand to see it all through – to catch the bus, to browse the shelves. It is as if, in her very heart, she knows. She knows that just as she played shops with the woman sitting beside her when that woman was a child, now they are playing the old game again.

But it is not just mundane things like shopping that they do together. No, sometimes Dianne will take her mother's hands and say, 'Let's dance!' And, in a moment, a bed has become a ballroom and Anne is twirling around a crowded dance floor with admirers who can only hope that the next waltz will be theirs.

And suddenly I know full well what is happening. It is all too apparent: apparent as the younger woman lifts the spoon to old lips, clear as day as Dianne wipes the food from the front of the new cardigan and fondles the face with the almost cheeky smile. Time has played its great trick and the roles have changed. The child is now the mother, and the mother the daughter.

And so it goes on. The child who was so often tucked in at night now plumps the pillows and tucks the blankets around her mother. 'Shall we say prayers before I go?' asks Dianne and she begins the opening words of the Lord's Prayer. What happens next never changes and never ceases to amaze me. Old lips, that for the last hour could not speak half a dozen words together that made any sense, now recite word perfect every syllable: 'Our Father who art in heaven . . .' It is as if deep in not just her mind but her spirit, is a part that even the Alzheimer's cannot reach. And the voice gets stronger as the prayer goes on – right to the very end: 'For thine is the kingdom and the power and the glory, for ever and ever. Amen.'

Dianne and I sit in the car together outside and she cries. But they are not tears of despair, because we both know what we have witnessed. It is as if an old lady has taken all the years of theology (of teaching that said, 'In the twinkling of an eye . . . we will be changed. For the perishable must clothe itself with the imperishable, and the mortal with immortality . . .'), shaken the dust off it and said to us, 'It is true – it is all true. There is a part of me that no disease, or even death, can rob me of. And one day you will visit me again and my face will light up when you walk into the room, but this time I will shout out loud, 'Dianne – it's you! Let's dance!' And we will.

The only way we can tell if we are valued and loved is by what people say and do. Love says, 'This is how much I appreciate you, and even if love seems hard to feel at the moment, as an act of the will, I will appreciate you.' When we are valued like that, it is life-changing. It affects our very personalities because it answers the deepest question a man or woman can ask: 'Do I have real worth?'

This is so clearly illustrated in one of the stories I like best. It's from a culture that seems strange to us, but the lesson at the heart of it is universal.

Johnny Lingo and the eight-cow wife

THE TIME I sailed to Kiniwata, an island off the Japanese coast, I took along a notebook. After I got back, it was filled with descriptions of the flora and fauna, native customs and costumes. But the only note that still interests me is the one that says: 'Johnny Lingo gave eight cows to Sarita's father.' But I don't need to have it in writing. I'm reminded of it every time I see a woman belittling her husband or a wife withering under her husband's scorn. I want to say to them, 'You should know why Johnny Lingo paid eight cows for his wife.'

Johnny Lingo wasn't exactly his name. But that's what Shenkin, the manager of the guest-house on Kiniwata, called him. Shenkin was from Chicago and had a habit of Americanising the names of the islanders.

But Johnny was mentioned by many people in many connections.

If I wanted to spend a few days on the neighbouring island of Nurabandi, Johnny Lingo could put me up. If I wanted to fish, he could show me where the biting was best. If it was pearls I sought, he would bring me the best buys. The people of Kiniwata all spoke highly of Johnny Lingo. Yet when they spoke, they smiled, and the smiles were slightly mocking. 'Get Johnny Lingo to help you find what you want and let him do the bargaining,' advised Shenkin. 'Johnny knows how to make a deal.'

'Johnny Lingo!' A boy seated nearby hooted the name and rocked with laughter.

'What's going on?' I demanded. 'Everyone tells me to get in touch with Johnny Lingo, then falls about laughing. Let me in on the joke.'

'Oh, the people like to laugh,' Shenkin said shrugging. 'Johnny's the brightest, the strongest young man on the islands. And, for his age, the richest.'

'But if he's all you say, what is there to laugh about?'

'Only one thing. Five months ago, at the festival, Johnny came to Kiniwata and found himself a wife. He paid her father eight cows.' I knew enough about island customs to be impressed. Two or three cows would buy a fair to middling wife, four or five a highly satisfactory one.

'Eight cows!' I said. 'She must have beauty that takes your breath away.'

'She's not ugly,' he conceded, and smiled a little. 'But the kindest could only call Sarita plain. Sam Karoo, her father, was afraid she'd be left on his hands.'

'But then he got eight cows for her? Isn't that extraordinary?'

'Never been paid before.'

'Yet you call Johnny's wife plain?'

'I said it would be a kindness to call her plain. She was skinny. She walked with her shoulders hunched and her head ducked. She was scared of her own shadow.'

'Well,' I said, 'I guess there's no accounting for love.'

'True enough,' agreed the man. 'And that's why the villagers grin when they talk about Johnny. They get special satisfaction from the fact that the sharpest trader in the islands was outwitted by dull old Sam Karoo.'

'But how?'

'No one knows and everyone wonders. All the cousins were urging Sam to ask for three cows and hold out for two until he was sure Johnny'd pay only one. Then Johnny came to Sam Karoo and said, 'Father of Sarita, I offer eight cows for your daughter.'

'Eight cows.' I murmured, 'I'd like to meet this Johnny Lingo.'

I wanted fish. I wanted pearls. So the next afternoon

I beached my boat at Nurabandi. And I noticed as I asked directions to Johnny's house that his name brought no sly smile to the lips of his fellow Nurabandians. And when I met the slim, serious young man, when he welcomed me with grace to his home, I was glad that from his own people he had respect unmingled with mockery. We sat in his house and talked. Then he asked, 'You come here from Kiniwata?'

'Yes. They say there's nothing I might want that you can't help me to get.'

He smiled gently. 'My wife is from Kiniwata.'

'Yes, I know.'

'They speak of her?'

'A little.'

'What do they say?'

'Why just . . .' The question caught me off balance. 'They told me you were married at festival time.'

'Nothing more?' The curve of his eyebrow told me he knew there had to be more.

'They also say the marriage settlement was eight cows.' I paused. 'They wonder why.'

'They ask that?' His eyes lighted with pleasure. 'Everyone in Kiniwata knows about the eight cows?'

I nodded.

'And in Nurabandi everyone knows it, too.' His chest expanded with satisfaction. 'Always and for ever, when they speak of marriage settlement, it will be remembered that Johnny Lingo paid eight cows for Sarita.'

So that's it, I thought: vanity.

And then I saw her. I watched her enter the room to place flowers on the table. She stood still a moment to smile at the young man beside me. Then she went swiftly out again. She was the most beautiful woman I have ever seen. The lift of her shoulders, the tilt of her chin, the sparkle of her eyes all spelt a pride to which no one could deny her the right.

I turned back to Johnny Lingo and found him looking at me.

'You admire her?' he murmured.

'She . . . she's glorious. But she is not Sarita from Kiniwata,' I said.

'There's only one Sarita. Perhaps she does not look the way they say she looked in Kiniwata.'

'She doesn't. I heard she was plain. They all make fun of you because you let yourself be cheated by Sam Karoo.'

'You think eight cows were too many?' A smile slid over his lips.

'No. But how can she be so different?'

'Do you ever think,' he asked, 'what it must mean to a woman to know that her husband has settled on the lowest price for which she can be bought? And then later, when the women talk, they boast of what their husbands paid for them. One says four cows, another maybe six. How does she feel, the woman who was sold for one or two? This could not happen to my Sarita.'

'Then you did this just to make your wife happy?'

'I wanted Sarita to be happy, yes. But I wanted more than that. You say she is different. This is true. Many things can change a woman. Things that happen inside, things that happen outside. But the thing that matters most is what she thinks about herself. In Kiniwata, Sarita believed she was worth nothing. Now she knows she is worth more than any other woman in the islands.'

'Then you wanted . . .'

'I wanted to marry Sarita. I loved her and no other woman.'

'But . . .' I was close to understanding.

'But,' he finished softly, 'I wanted an eight-cow wife.'[8]

For most of my life, I have been involved in some kind of leadership — business, church, charities. One of the most powerful things that can happen in a team is when they not only work together, but actually look out for each other.

A few geese . . . and a lesson on team work

ONE OF THE world's marvels is the migratory cycle of birds. Take the Arctic tern, for example. When scientists added up the total distance flown by one of these birds during its lifetime, they found it equalled three round trips to the moon – more than 1.25 million miles!

Geese are another long-distance migratory bird. Next autumn, when you see the geese heading south for the winter, flying along in a V-shaped formation, you might consider what science has discovered as to why they fly that way. As each bird flaps its wings, it creates an uplift for the bird immediately following. By flying in a V-formation the whole flock adds at least 70 per cent more to its flying range than if each bird were flying on its own.

When a goose falls out of formation, it suddenly feels the drag and resistance of trying to go it alone and quickly gets back into formation to take advantage of the lifting power of the bird in front.

When the leading goose gets tired, it slips to the back and another goose flies point. It is sensible to take turns doing demanding jobs – whether with people or with geese flying south. Geese honk from behind to encourage those up front to keep up their speed.

When a goose gets sick or is wounded by gunshot and falls out of formation, one or two of the other geese fall out with it and follow it down to lend help and protection. They stay with the fallen goose until it is able to fly or until it dies. Only then do they launch out on their own, or with another formation, to catch up with their group.

People who share a common direction and sense of community can get where they are going much more quickly and easily because they are travelling on the thrust of one another's efforts. If we have as much sense as a goose, we will stay in formation with those who are headed the same way we are. If we have the sense of a goose, we will stand by each other when danger threatens or trouble comes.

One of the reasons why many people have never seen their dreams realised is that they share them with the wrong people. You may be one of those. You ran to your boss, friends or family full of your new idea, bursting with the possibility of the dream, but little did you know that the bucket of cold water was already waiting behind the door. There have been times in my life when I have been part of the answer to people realising their dreams and, sadly, occasions when I have been part of the problem. Let me tell you about one of the latter.

Chasing the dream

I WAS A LAWYER in my mid-thirties when I stood with Rob and his wife, Jennie, in front of a plot of land. He was disabled; in fact, he had been in a wheelchair for over ten years, and they were drawing social security benefit. They told me they had a dream to build a holiday centre for disabled people. Rob said, 'I want to build an adventure park for disabled kids. Kids in wheelchairs need to take risks as much as other kids, even if they fall out of the wheelchair once in a while.'

I asked them how much money they had; they told me it was almost nothing – certainly nowhere near enough to even contemplate such a project. I warned them about having unrealistic goals. They were disappointed but polite and thanked me for my time and advice. Perhaps

I'd annoyed them, but the second they left my office they got started on their dream.

She got a job as a nurse; he began making furniture and selling it to friends and family. Eventually they bought a tiny terraced house that was, in estate agent's language, 'in need of some modernisation'. They lived on a pittance and used every penny to improve their new property. They worked on that house night and day and eventually sold it for a good profit. Afterwards, they bought a piece of land and begged and borrowed materials, advice and help from whoever would give it. They designed and built a house in which disabled and able people could live together in comfort. A major magazine ran regular features as the property progressed. After three years, they sold it and ploughed the money straight into their dream.

We sometimes say that we know where we were when we heard the news of certain deaths – think of John F. Kennedy or Princess Diana, for instance. I was in a corner shop when I got the news that Rob had died. It's true that he died too young – but not before thousands of kids had spent holidays on the farm he created just for them; not before they had fed the chickens, milked the goats, and occasionally fallen out of their wheelchairs on the adventure course; not before the government appointed him as an advisor on housing and programmes for disabled people; and not before he saw – and caught – his dream.

I've discovered that there are moments when an audience and the storyteller become one — they are experiencing the story together. *Occasionally, I decide to tell a story that costs me emotionally each time I relate it, and I've wondered sometimes whether it is too personal — the memories it evokes are too painful. But often, when I do tell those stories, I feel the audience not only understands that pain but, in some mystical way, even shares it.*

No regrets

I WAS ON A speaking tour in South Africa and had just got off a plane in Johannesburg when I switched on my mobile phone and saw a text message asking me to ring home immediately. I made the call during the short bus ride from the plane to the terminal and discovered that my good and dear friend, Bob, had died in his sleep. His death was both sudden and unexpected: he was not old, nor, to my knowledge, ill. I bent over in a corner of the baggage reclaim area and cried helplessly.

Bob was a builder. Yes, I know what you're thinking – and he enjoyed the joke as well. Forgive me if you are a builder, but Bob was a typical builder: when you showed him a job you wanted done, he would always go through the same routine. He'd look around the room, stare up at the ceiling, examine the walls, go outside, look at the roof and then purse his lips, suck in a breath of air and say, 'Who did this work for you? It's terrible!' And I would reply, 'You did, Bob.' And he would blush, shrug his shoulders and say, 'Ah, well, it was a long time ago . . .'

Four of us used to play snooker together. On the wall of the snooker room was a chalkboard where we kept a record of the highest score ever achieved among us. That figure had not changed for almost five years: 35. When I returned from South Africa I went back to the room where we used to play and noticed that after our last game, Bob had sneaked back and written on the chalkboard: Bob – 146. Was he just too humble to claim a perfect score of 147? We'll never know, but we've decided that Bob's joke will never be erased.

I can honestly tell you that I had never felt grief like this. And although I cried a lot, I almost felt as if I should be crying more. Often I found myself shaking my head in disbelief. Sometimes I could almost hear his voice; I half expected him to saunter into the room and say, 'You are doomed tonight! I've brought my new snooker cue with me.' Once I actually pinched myself to be sure that it was not some dreadful nightmare from which I could mercifully wake.

In C. S. Lewis's *A Grief Observed*, Lewis deals with the fact that grief often comes in waves – and keeps coming. He puts it like this:

In grief nothing 'stays put'. One keeps on emerging from a phase, but it always recurs . . . Will it be for always? How often will the vast emptiness astonish me like a complete novelty and make me say, 'I never realised my loss until this moment?' . . . They say the coward dies many times; so does the beloved.

But there is at least this consolation: there are no regrets. I may not be able to say that about every friend who might die suddenly, but I can say it about Bob. Did we ever hurt each other? Yes – but like a grouchy old couple we eventually made up. Did we take time simply to laugh together? Yes – I have a hundred memories of silliness. But perhaps above all, we told each other now and then how much our friendship mattered.

The other day I spoke to five hundred men at a conference. I told them about Bob and I urged them to tell their friends that they were appreciated and valued – loved even. As the words came out of my mouth, I realised that it was an unusual thing to say to a bunch of blokes.

I know you may not be the emotional kind, but trust me on this. Even if it means you have to move way out of your comfort zone, you will not regret that you not only loved someone – but that you told them so.

Just don't leave it too late.

I picked up the phone, scrolled to Katie's number and pressed enter. It rang for a few seconds before she answered. 'All well, Kate?' There was a pause and then she said, 'I don't feel so good, Dad.' And so began one of the darkest periods of our family life.

Held by God

KATIE, MY DAUGHTER, went into hospital for a routine operation a couple of years ago. The next day she developed complications, and over the following couple of weeks she had two further major operations, a blood transfusion and a suspected heart attack.

Katie and her husband, Paul, have two small children, and when Paul couldn't be at her bedside, I took his place – often sitting for hours just watching her sleeping, with tubes seemingly coming out of every part of her body. Dianne had gone in for a hip-replacement operation the day before Katie was admitted, so she too was in hospital – albeit a different one, fifteen miles away.

When I visited Dianne we would talk together, but Katie couldn't do that. I don't like sitting still, yet I found it strangely easy to simply *be* by that bedside, watching her and praying. Over the years, I have seen life traumas affect people's faith in such different ways. Some have said, 'There can't be a God who loves me. If there was, he wouldn't let me go through this.' I understand that reaction.

Another reaction is a bit less clear-cut and goes something like this: 'God, I don't really understand any of this. I know that if you said just one word you could put it all right this very second, though I also know that doesn't always happen. But whatever *does* happen, I need you more than ever. Please make this terror go away, but in it, and through it, and even if the very worst happens, please hold me in this darkness.'

Mine was the second reaction. I don't think it was because I am any more spiritual than others who had the first response; it is simply that as I sat by Katie's bed, I realised that it all came down to one simple question: 'Do I trust God?'

What I found myself asking was: 'Do I trust God to somehow keep holding us all – whatever happens?' And I discovered that I did. That discovery was almost a surprise – a bit like the old poet in the Psalms saying, 'If I go up to the heavens, you are there. If I make my bed in the depths, you are there . . . Even there . . . your right hand will hold me fast.'[9] In other words, 'I really didn't expect to find you *here*!'

Just before Katie was born, I waited outside an operating theatre as Dianne gave birth by Caesarean section. I remember it so vividly. I desperately wanted a boy. Suddenly I heard a cry, and then the door opened and the midwife handed me a tiny bundle. She said, 'You've got a lovely daughter.' My heart sank. And then she pulled aside the blanket that was covering the baby's face and I looked into Katie's eyes. And at that moment I fell in love – and have been so ever since.

Many years have subsequently passed, but as I waited in that same hospital and responded to Katie's tentative wave as she was wheeled into the operating theatre, I realised that although she was now a woman with a family of her own, here I was, still trying to be a father to her.

One night Katie had just come back to the recovery ward after a major operation – it was almost midnight. Paul and I were standing by her bed and, as we were about to leave, Katie asked the nurse who was attending her if she could have a moment alone with just Paul and me. 'Of course, my dear,' said the nurse. Katie looked up at me and said, 'Dad, would you say a prayer?'

When Katie and Lloyd were small children, we used to say the same little prayer with them each night. Now I said the old prayer again – not with the child, but with the woman, a mother herself.

Lord, keep us safe this night,
Secure from all our fears,
May angels guard us while we sleep,
'Til morning light appears.

P.S. Katie is well now.

The radio interview had nearly come to an end and the presenter asked me his closing question: 'What do you believe to be the greatest threat to relationships and the stability of family life?' In milliseconds, my mind went back to a summer day the year before and I knew what my answer would be.

January love

IT IS THE wedding day of my friend's daughter and I have been asked to say a few words at the service. In many ways, this is a perfect day: the bride looks wonderful; the groom is like a handsome prince; the sun is streaming through the stained glass windows of the old church. As I sit waiting for my own part in the service, I watch the young couple. I can see they have eyes and ears only for each other. I sigh inwardly and tell myself that in such circumstances I would be wise not to take myself too seriously; for them, listening to this old guy for a few minutes is part of the deal – and, hopefully, a part that will soon be over.

I consider what I intend to say and debate whether or not I dare speak about the issue that's on my mind. As I am still thinking, I hear my name announced and I rise from my seat to go to the front of the little church. Even as I walk, I am wondering if I dare mention it and then, quite suddenly, I decide.

'I want to talk to you today about January love,' I say. 'I often go to write my books in a small cottage in West Wales. One August afternoon, I took a break and went for a walk on the beach. It was a wonderful day. The sun shone out of a cloudless sky. Behind me, part-framing the bay, were patchwork hills, and in front of me the sea shimmered in the summer heat. It felt good to be alive. I walked along the beach, then made my way back to the cottage. As I neared it, I saw an old fisherman sitting on a bench. "It's glorious, isn't it?" I said. I don't know if he was having a bad day or was just tired of tourists, but he said, "You should see it in January."

'The next day I walked on the beach again. It looked as lovely as it had twenty-four hours earlier, but this time I imagined the hills, the bay and the sea whisper to me, "Will you love us in January?"'

If the course of married life has seasons, then most begin in summer. These are days filled with warmth when we not only say we are in love, but we *feel* in love. Of course, to love in summer is relatively easy, but marriages that are to last have a much harsher test ahead: it is the challenge of 'January love' – of surviving the winter of our relationship. And just as the first chill winds of autumn may catch us by surprise, so a change in the climate of a relationship can be devastating. Whereas our relationship in summer was characterised by warm breezes, we find that biting winds now test our love. These are dark and cold days, but there is no relationship that does not, at some time, have to love in January – love, at least for a while, not 'because of' but 'in spite of'. Marriages break up, relationships fail – those things are facts of life. But it's also a fact that we will never find a lasting relationship with anybody unless we are prepared at times to fight to keep our love alive.

I remember counselling a couple in their mid-twenties; she was cradling a six-month-old baby girl in her arms; they were about to divorce. I asked the man why he was leaving his wife. He said, 'I don't feel in love any more.' I said, 'Did anybody ever tell you that the feelings of love often go up and down – that this is normal? Did anybody ever say that sometimes you have to love not just with the heart but, at least for a time, with the *will*? Did anybody ever tell you that it's not uncommon after the birth of a little one for the relationship to be a bit strained – perhaps the sex isn't so good for a time, perhaps you are rowing a bit more than usual? Did nobody ever tell you about January love?' He looked at me and said, 'No, nobody told me that.'

As he spoke, I couldn't help but gaze at his little girl lying fast asleep in her mother's arms, and I wondered what the future held for this new family, soon to break apart. I know it's not possible or even desirable to keep every relationship together, but perhaps *this* relationship could have been saved, even with just a little understanding of something as simple as January love.

But nobody had told him that.

After speaking to hundreds of thousands of parents in different cultures across the world I've discovered that the last thing people need to hear is clever answers. Although, of course, we want answers to the problems we are experiencing, almost as much as that, we need to know we are not alone. In fact, we can often find our own solutions, so long as we know that we're not the worst mother or father on the face of the earth; that other parents have gone down the same road – and survived. Humour is a great way of getting this message across. I often tell this little piece to parents in our seminars.

Ready for parenthood?

WHY DIDN'T ANYBODY prepare us for having babies? One parent devised some simple tests to see if expectant parents are ready.[10] Here are a few of them.

1. To prepare for pregnancy: Women: put on a dressing gown and stick a beanbag down the front. Leave it there. After nine months, take out 10 per cent of the beans.
2. To prepare for having children: Men: go to the local chemist, tip the contents of your wallet onto the counter and tell the pharmacist to help himself. Then go to the supermarket. Arrange to have your salary paid directly to their head office. Go home. Pick up the newspaper. Read it for the last time.

3. Dealing with mess: To find out if you can deal with the mess small children make, smear peanut butter onto the sofa and jam onto the curtains. Hide a fish finger behind the stereo and leave it there all summer. Stick your fingers in the flowerbeds and then rub them on the clean walls. Cover the stains with crayon. How does that look?

4. Feeding children: To test your ability to carry out feeding a twelve-month-old baby, hollow out a melon. Make a small hole in the side. Suspend the melon from the ceiling and swing it from side to side. Now get a bowl of soggy cornflakes and attempt to spoon them into the swaying melon while pretending to be an aeroplane. Continue until half the cornflakes are gone. Tip the rest into your lap, making sure that a lot of it falls on the floor.

5. Getting children dressed: To test your ability to dress small children, buy a live octopus and a string bag. Attempt to put the octopus into the string bag so that no arms hang out. Time allowed: five minutes.

6. Going out in the car: Make a recording of someone shouting 'Mummy!' or 'Daddy' repeatedly. Important Note: there must be no more than a four-second delay between each 'Mummy/Daddy'. Include occasional crescendo to the level of a

supersonic jet. Play this tape in your car everywhere you go for the next four years. You are now ready to take a long trip with a toddler.

7. Watching TV: Learn the names of every character from *Bing, Rosie and Jim, Teletubbies* and *Postman Pat*. Watch nothing else on television for at least five years.

8. Cars: Forget the BMW. Buy a practical five-door wagon. Buy a chocolate ice cream cone and put it in the glove compartment. Leave it there. Get a coin. Insert it into the CD player. Take a box of chocolate biscuits; mash them into the back seat. Run a garden rake along both sides of the car.

9. Grocery shopping: Go to the local supermarket. Take with you the nearest thing you can find to a pre-school child – a fully-grown goat is excellent. If you intend to have more than one child, take more than one goat. Buy your weekly groceries without letting the goat(s) out of your sight. Pay for everything the goat eats or destroys. Until you can easily accomplish this, do not even contemplate having children.

I wrote a book called The Heart of Success *some years ago. It did pretty well — it got on the* Sunday Times *bestseller list for business books — and I received lots of invitations from blue chip companies to talk about the principles I cover in it. (One unusual engagement was to address the President of Swaziland and his whole cabinet for an hour!) As you may imagine, many of those in the audience at these events may be extremely successful, wealthy and powerful. I often smile inside, watching them take notes as I share lessons I learnt from somebody who was none of those things.*

The postman

MY FATHER WAS a postman. He joined what was then the General Post Office as a fourteen-year-old boy repairing the wiring at the top of telegraph poles and went on to deliver letters for the rest of his working life. He was bright – very bright – and when he came back from the Second World War the authorities in the postal service asked him to train for management. But whatever it was, when he got home in 1945 he didn't want any hassle; he wasn't looking for glory, he just wanted to provide for his family the best way he could. And he wanted to deliver letters.

My father sometimes worked a night shift as a sorter of mail. Some evenings, as I was trying to extend bedtime, I would watch him getting ready. In those days we didn't have a bathroom; all the washing there was – whether dishes, clothes or bodies – was done in a large stone kitchen sink. He always followed the same routine: first, he would lay out his uniform, then he would shave and wash, and, finally, he would clean his shoes.

My father's shoes always shone. One day when I was about eight or nine, I caught him cleaning the soles. I said, 'Don't do that, Dad. It's a waste of time. Nobody will ever know.' He looked up at me and said, '*I'll* know.'

The years went by and the time came when I had to leave the small primary school where all my friends from our street went and join the grammar school. It was another world to me. I remember once the teacher asked us to shout out what our fathers did for a living. The boy next to me yelled out, 'Company director'. I can remember whispering, 'Postman' as quietly as I could.

One night when my father was getting ready for work, I interrupted him. 'Don't you ever get bored of just pushing letters through doors?' If I hurt him, he didn't show it. He said, 'Son, your father delivers the Royal Mail.' He made it sound as if the Queen herself had asked him to do it. 'People rely on me – businesses, armies and police forces, friends and relatives from overseas. I deliver all their letters. You should come with me some day and see somebody waiting at their door to see if I've got a letter for them. It may be about a job they've been hoping for, a letter from a daughter they haven't heard from for a while, or perhaps just a birthday card. No, Son, I don't get bored.'

He delivered letters for forty-six years. In all that time, he had only eleven days' absence due to sickness, and when he retired the Queen gave him a medal: it was for delivering the Royal Mail.

I was lecturing in Moscow when I got the news that he was dying. I just managed to catch an overnight flight back and as the plane made its way across the night sky above Europe, my mind was going back over my memories of this man; over things I would have liked to have said to him and a couple I wish I hadn't. But above all, I was trying again to understand him. When I landed, it was in the early hours of the morning. A friend was waiting to drive me home. 'How's my dad?' I asked him. 'I'm sorry,' he said, 'your father died a couple of hours ago.'

I remember walking into his room and looking at him. I almost expected him to say some old familiar phrase, and yet he was still, in so many ways, an enigma to me. He was poor and yet he was never in debt. He had few possessions and yet he was the most content man I have ever met. I can't remember him ever telling me he loved me and yet I'm sure that he did. He did none of the things that I have written about in *The Sixty Minute Father* – he didn't play with us, hug us, or praise us much. But he did give us complete and utter security. And he was always there.

The other night I woke at about 2.30 a.m. and couldn't get back to sleep. I wandered into my study and began flicking through the books on the shelves, and then my eyes fell upon a large brown envelope. It contained the contents of a box that my father kept in his cupboard and I began to sift through documents I hadn't really looked at since his death. Some papers in a special bundle were both fascinating and frustrating. Fascinating because they opened a window into part of my father's life that I know almost nothing of, and frustrating because it was *just a window*. He wasn't much of a communicator. He would go out once a week on a Saturday night, have a few beers, and when he returned he would talk. But by the Sunday morning he was back in his shell again. There were lots of things I would have wanted to ask him, and even now I have so many questions.

At the front of the bundle was a signed card from Field Marshal Montgomery: 'I feel I cannot let you leave 21 Army Group without a message of thanks and farewell.' Just behind that was a soldier's service and pay book. It noted that he was a postman before he enlisted, that he was a special operator, was gassed in September 1941 and decorated three years later. He had told us none of this.

I knew that he had been in France, but what had he

seen, what had he done – and what did it mean that his commanding officer had written on his release certificate: 'This man has worked under difficult conditions'? I contacted the Army Records Office and they told me that my father, as a Morse code operator, was involved in some kind of 'special operations'.

Which was the real man? The character huddled over the Morse code machine, most likely behind enemy lines in France, or the figure pounding the streets with his sack on his back? Probably both. I do know this: whatever he did, he did with all his heart.

The best way I can describe him is to say that he had dignity. You can't buy that. You can't guarantee it by education or social status. And because he had that dignity, he owed it to himself to do whatever job he did as well as he could.

That's why my father cleaned the soles of his shoes.

Where do we find examples of unconditional love? In my experience, it is so often among those who parent children with special needs. These parents face the most difficult of circumstances, often with little help or understanding. They do not want anybody to romanticise the task they do; nevertheless, in the everyday challenges, in the bearing of the misunderstanding of others, and in the knowledge that this is a lifelong commitment, they constantly demonstrate an unconditional love.

I received a quite remarkable letter from a mother. She'd been told that she would never be able to conceive, but years later gave birth to a daughter. I felt I had to speak to her and we had a wonderful telephone conversation: she urged me to always remember the parents of children with disabilities – for they carry, as she put it, 'A responsibility, a love and a pain that is hard to convey to those who have never been there.' This is her story.

The promise

WHEN MY DAUGHTER Kelly was born, I was told that she was blind, almost certainly intellectually impaired, and with severely dysfunctional internal organs.

I will never forget holding this precious child in a shawl and, with tears running down my face, wondering what the future held for her. As I gazed down at her, she looked so vulnerable, and emotion after emotion was flooding through me. I suddenly had a compelling desire to commit my feelings to paper. When she was just seven weeks old I wrote my daughter a letter. I have kept it in a drawer since the day I wrote it all those years ago. If you think it would help others, please use it.

My darling Kelly,

As I write, you are seven weeks old, a very beautiful baby, and unspeakably precious to your father and me. When you were born, it was wonderful to have you, a little daughter. Now, with the news that you are blind, we love you with an even more tender love.

I have wept for you, Kelly, these last days, as I've remembered experiences that you will never have. But I am also deeply sure that all is well and there is nothing to be afraid of in the future.

God's hand is on you and he will shape and fashion you, often through heartache and pain, into an exceptional woman. You are very special to us.

Kelly, I want you to be the best that you can be. Don't ever settle for second best, making your disability an excuse not to be excellent. Be brave and full of laughter. Listen with your ears and your heart to others, always seeking to bring healing and love to them. Be strong and unrelenting in your desire to live life to its fullest. Many precious things will be withheld from you, but the best will always be there for you. Trust God.

My sweet child, I love you so much and I promise to be with you as you grow – in understanding, encouragement, in discipline and in tenderness.

Your mother,
Elizabeth Thomas

A promise to be with you as you grow – in understanding, encouragement, discipline and tenderness.

No child could ask more from a mother.

I have written a number of Sixty Minute *books* (The Sixty Minute Father, . . . Mother, . . . Marriage, . . . Family, . . . Grandparent *and* . . . Debtbuster) *and they have all been important to me, but perhaps because I am a little older, it's another sixty minutes that recently got my attention.*

The last sixty minutes

I HAD A DREAM. I was in heaven – in a waiting room. At any minute, I would be called into the big room along the corridor for the review of my life. As I sat there, it wasn't the memory of my death that bothered me (although I could remember stepping off the kerb and seeing a little grey van at the last moment), it was something else.

Countless preachers on earth had assured me that in heaven there were no negative emotions – just all the good stuff. Well, I can tell you that either they were all wrong or I wasn't in heaven because, as I watched people being called in one by one for their interview, I was scared stiff. It wasn't that I thought I'd be unmasked and immediately dispatched from the celestial city; I'd long ago come to believe that if I ever got there it would be because of what *he* had done, not me. So why was I so afraid?

I was scared because on earth it had been easy to talk about the wonders of heaven and the joy of meeting the master himself, but now it was different: I was actually going to be face to face with him. And in my heart I realised that all the stuff that had convinced me I'd been a pretty good bloke in life wouldn't count for so much in that room because he *really* knew all about me. On earth, I'd known the things that mattered to him, but it had been so easy to forget them.

And then it happened. I don't know if the woman who walked into the waiting room was an angel, but she was certainly one to me. 'I'm sorry, but we're running late,' she whispered. 'If you want to, you can go back to earth for sixty minutes. I'm afraid that after that you will step off the kerb again, but you will have one hour before you return for your one-to-one.' I practically hugged her. I ran out of the room and found myself standing again on the edge of a busy road.

Sixty minutes. I spent the first five panicking about how best to use the time, but then a strange peace settled on me. Finding a corner table in my familiar old coffee shop, I ordered a full-fat latte (what harm could it do now?) and started to phone people. I rang Charles first. He seemed surprised to hear from me. 'Charles,' I blurted out, 'I don't have long to talk, but I want you to know that I'm sorry. I was wrong. Please forgive me.' A silence ate up at least ten seconds of my precious time, but then I heard him say, 'I do forgive you – gladly.'

My next call was harder – much harder. 'Sophie, it's me. Sophie, I can't say you didn't hurt me, but I want you to know that with every fibre in my body, I forgive you.'

My phone was hot now. 'Jack, I love you.' 'Suzie, I love you.' 'Tommy, you have been an incredible friend.' My wife, my kids, and friends – some I hadn't seen for thirty years and a few I'd treated badly – I spoke to them all.

As I left the coffee shop it was getting dark. I had two minutes left. A man selling *The Big Issue* was packing up outside. 'How many magazines have you got left?' I asked. 'Six, mate – I haven't sold one in the last two hours.' I thrust a £20 note into his hand, 'I'll take them all!'

I looked at my watch – ten seconds left. I got to the kerb and glanced back. *The Big Issue* man was looking at me – right into my eyes – as if he knew me. And he was smiling.

A small grey van was coming around the bend of the road.

I made a bad mistake. I realise that, in itself, this isn't earth-shattering news, but this was a really *bad mistake. And I didn't realise it for over a week.*

Judge not, lest . . .

ONCE A MONTH I chair a meeting of about forty people. It starts at 9.00 a.m., but recently I'd noticed that people were arriving late. By the time we were due to begin, there were sometimes just a handful in the room and then the rest dribbled in over the next ten minutes or so. Now obviously that's wrong, and I could have been forgiven for asking them to make every effort to be punctual, but that's not what I did.

As I opened the meeting and gazed out on the faithful few who were there on time, I had a bright idea. I said, 'As latecomers arrive, let's give them a round of applause!' And so we did. The first unfortunate, who arrived only a minute late, looked surprised to be welcomed with such enthusiasm and then, as the penny dropped, slipped into a seat, red-faced. There was a little flurry at 9.05, vigorous applause for the three stragglers who were seven minutes late, and by the time the poor soul – who'd no doubt already had a bad day – tried to sneak in at the back at 9.10 we were clapping as if it were the last night at the Proms.

How we laughed! I felt pleased with myself – a bit of fun and a lesson taught. Afterwards I spoke to those I'd embarrassed and reassured them that 'It wasn't just you' and 'It was just a bit of fun', although secretly I felt delighted with my little strategy. There was only one fly in the ointment. When we had finished clapping the last person, somebody shouted out some words of Jesus: 'Do not judge, or you too will be judged.'

To be honest, I was enjoying my little ruse and feeling so pleased with myself that I hardly heard them. But over the next few days those words gnawed quietly at my brain and at 7.20 a.m., exactly one week after the incident, they exploded into dreadful realisation. Two things happened almost at once. First, I remembered how that quote ended: 'For in the same way you judge others, you will be judged.' Second, I realised I was running late!

By the time I'd put my underpants on backwards, skipped the shower and used Dianne's hairspray instead of deodorant, I was a wreck. I drove like a maniac, rushed up the stairs to the meeting room, and made it with thirty seconds to spare. But even as I sat smelling of Elnett, I realised that this was now my life. Every month I was condemned to the dreadful potential of being the one clapped into the meeting – accused now not only of lateness, but of hypocrisy.

I have thought so much about this in the intervening weeks. In fact, next week I will apologise to the group, not only because I now realise I was wrong, but for a much more selfish motive. I don't want people – friends, work colleagues, spouses, even children – to judge me as I judge others.

If you want to, you can choose to go through life pointing out where others get things wrong, complaining every time somebody upsets you, constantly holding others to account, exercising your 'rights' and even letting people know when they're late.

Just get used to wearing your pants on backwards.

Why do some experiences in life affect us so profoundly? In themselves, they don't seem particularly special or unusual, and yet they practically touch our very souls. Perhaps it's because they evoke memories and emotions in us that have long since lain dormant — but who really knows the reason? Let me tell you about a very ordinary school photograph that made me cry.

Pick me!

THE CLASS PHOTOGRAPH was of a large group of children at the beginning of their teen years. The girls were already looking like women in the making, the boys were looking like – well, large boys. But one girl caught my attention. She was very overweight and sat with her hands on her knees. She did not have a pretty face and she smiled out from behind thick spectacles. I asked my friend's child to tell me about her.

Apparently, she had few friends because, among other things, she smelt a little and some of the children would not sit by her. She was not good at sport and regularly came somewhere near the bottom of the class in terms of academic achievement. Whenever the teacher asked two leaders to pick teams, she was always the last one chosen, and invariably one captain would say, 'You can have her.'

As I looked at her, I felt a great emotion well up in me. I wanted to hug her, to tell her that she was *somebody*. I wanted to find something in that child's life that she could do moderately well and praise her for it. I wanted to tell her that I would always be her friend and that I would love to sit by her.

Not long ago I came across this little poem:[11]

Picking Teams

When we pick teams in the playground,
Whatever the game might be,
There's always somebody left till last,
And usually it's me.

I stand there looking hopeful,
And tapping myself on the chest,
But the captains pick the others first,
Starting of course with the best.

Maybe if teams were sometimes picked
Starting with the worst,
Once in his life a boy like me
Could end up being first.

There's a lovely line in the film *My Girl*. Two small children are sitting on a fence, dangling their legs in the air and discussing what heaven might be like. One says, 'When you play sports, there's no teams, *so nobody gets picked last.*'

Humourist Sam Levenson said that the reason grandparents and grandkids get along so well is that they've got a common enemy! Well, whether or not that's true, what is certain is that grandparents can make a big difference in a child's life. Here are a couple of little stories I like to tell about two who demonstrated this in a special way.

The gift of a grandparent

SOME TIME AGO, a friend of mine attended a school prize-giving – one with a difference. The school cared for severely physically and mentally disadvantaged children. The audience listened as the head read out the children's names and the reasons why these particular pupils had won a prize. 'Mark, because he has fed himself all this term', 'Richard, because he has learnt to wipe his bottom', and 'Susan, who has recited a poem and can brush her teeth.' As some shuffled and others danced to collect their trophies, there was hardly a dry eye in the place.

The last child to go to the rostrum had Down's syndrome as well as other physical challenges. The head read out the accreditation: 'Finally, a prize for Peter Harries, who is awarded most improved pupil of the year.' Peter was wheeled down the aisle towards the podium with his hands above his head in the traditional athletes' signal of triumph. As he reached the ramp at the foot of the podium a man sitting next to my friend suddenly stood and started cheering at the top of his voice. The audience responded in kind and by the time Peter reached the head teacher the place was going crazy. Finally, the prize was presented and the noise abated. As he sat down, the man whispered to my friend, 'He's my grandson.'

For all of us life can be testing, but what an asset it would be to face it with that sort of grandparent. That is, perhaps, why one child said, 'A grandfather is a little bit parent, a little bit teacher, and a little bit best friend.' The truth is that most of us – even as adults – crave somebody who looks for the best in us: someone to whom praise comes more quickly than criticism.

An elderly grandmother went to watch her grandson at the school Sports Day. Tom didn't get into the final of the 100 metres or the 200 metres, and he was unplaced in the longer races as well. In fact, the only event in which he looked remotely comfortable was the egg and spoon race, but even then he came last. As Tom and his grandmother walked away together, the little boy's head was down until she put her arm around him and whispered, 'You were the only one whose egg didn't fall off the spoon.' That young boy never did make it as a sportsman, but against the odds he did achieve great things in other areas of his life. I'm not surprised . . .

It's hard to fail with a grandmother like that.

Time is a fascinating thing – you can't buy it, mortgage it or even save it. When people say things like, 'I've saved an hour!', I want to reply, 'Really? Where did you put it?' You can save money – perhaps in a bank or even under the bed – but you can only spend *time. And although most people say they'd like to have* more *time, the problem is that everybody has all the time there is.*

Nobody ever said . . .

I WAS GIVEN SOME great advice once about how to manage the mound of paper that comes into our lives every day. With regard to the mail at home, my friend said, 'Always open it over a wastepaper bin. You will find you can rip up 90 per cent of it immediately and you'll know you've really got it under control when you rip it all up without opening any of it!' I try to remember what she said, but the other day a piece of junk mail got through the system.

Dear Underachiever,
    I'm not trying to insult you or demean you ['thank goodness he's not trying,' I think], I just happen to believe that most people are underachievers. These

unfulfilled men and women never reach their potential. I believe in being a 'no-limit' person, and I can make you one.

It was 7.00 a.m. I stood in the hallway of my home, bleary-eyed, letter in hand, gazing down at my slippers and wondering, 'Would I like to be a "no-limit" person? Would I like to be able to have a full-time job, sit on endless committees, learn crochet and Italian in my spare time, and still build a strong relationship with my wife and children? Would I like to say yes every time somebody asks me to do something and still have space for my own family? Do I wish that I was Superman and could fly and juggle at the same time?' You bet I do. But I can't.

And the reason I can't do it all is that time is limited. Whether I am rich or poor, clever or dull, I have exactly the same amount of time as everybody else. Each day comes to me full of 1,440 minutes. By the time I wake, realise that it's not Saturday but Monday, and get dressed, I have just 1,000 left. Every day I spend all of those minutes, and every choice I make as to how I will spend them precludes another option.

There is no shortage of time-saving devices, fast food and calendar apps that allow us to plan every minute of the day. The only thing we don't have any more of is time. But none of us would live our lives so full of hectic activity if we thought that it would always be like that – that there will never be time to build good relationships with our husband, wife, children or friends. So we fool ourselves that this is just a busy period of our lives and that when it is over we will have more time. We wait patiently for that elusive quieter day but, for most of us, it never comes.

When Katie was a little girl, I would read her a bedtime story. I remember that sometimes in the middle of the tale the phone would ring downstairs (the only phone in the house then). Like a lion that has sensed its prey, my ears would prick up immediately. Katie would say, 'Don't answer it, Dad. We're in the middle of the story.' I'd reply, 'I'll only be a minute, Kate – back in a jiff!'

Often that one call would lead to another and then another until I'd suddenly realise that half an hour had passed and I had left a princess stranded in a castle in the story. I would rush back upstairs and into Katie's room. The light would still be on, and the book would be lying open on the pillow next to her head, but little eyes had lost the fight to stay awake as long as they could.

I know it's not always possible to give our kids all the time we want, but can I share with you something I don't understand when I look back at that little scenario. I've had an interesting life. I've written over twenty books and have had the opportunity of speaking all over the world to individuals, companies and sometimes governments. When I was a lawyer I was involved in murder trials and business takeovers, and since leaving the legal practice, I have helped build a national charity. All those endeavours have meant my having thousands of business phone calls. Many of them have been described as 'Urgent' with the message, 'Please ring back ASAP.'

Do you know something? I can't remember one – not one – that couldn't have waited ten minutes while I finished a bedtime story. It's just that at the time, all those years ago, those calls seemed so very pressing . . . and I can't quite remember why.

One day it dawned on me that although I was relatively successful, my family were slipping through my fingers. Thankfully we made some fundamental changes in our family life. But three things kept me in that lifestyle far longer than they should have: first, I told myself that I was working long hours for *their* sakes. But one psychologist put it well: 'Sometimes we are so busy giving our children what we didn't have, we don't have time to give them what we *did* have.' Next, I forgot how fast the door of childhood closes – the days are long but the years are short. And last of all, I kidded myself that a slower day was coming.

I talked about those mistakes in *The Sixty Minute Father*. Wherever in the world that book is sold, people thank me for one line in particular. It urges us, while we are busy building careers, not to forget to invest time in building relationships with those we love. If we *don't* give time to this, we may be successful outside the home, but we will look back at our life with tremendous regret.

And the line? Oh, it's very simple:

Nobody ever said on their deathbed: 'I wish I'd spent more time at the office.'

There were times when Lloyd was a teenager (quite a few times, actually) when Dianne and I felt that our sanity was seriously under threat. In desperation one day, I decided to reread everything I had ever written about parenting. None of it helped a jot. (The truth is that when it comes to their own children there are no parenting experts — just people trying to get their kids through as best they can.) But as I was flicking through some papers, I came across a description of adolescence written by a well-known psychologist. Here is the way I retell it in our parenting events.

Come in, teenager! It's earth calling

A RENOWNED PSYCHOLOGIST HAS likened the teenage experience to the launch of a spacecraft. With twelve years or so of training behind him, a boy makes his way to the launch pad. He climbs aboard *Adolescent One* as his parents bite their nails at Mission Control. The engines roar into life and the boy rockets into the stratosphere. Then the parents lose all contact with the spaceship.

His mother is beside herself. Her son promised to ring when he got to the moon and, anyway, has he forgotten he's got a dental appointment next Tuesday? But there's no communication. Nothing. Well, not exactly nothing: the radio operator manages to pick up what sound like grunts, though nobody can decipher them.

The years go by, then, suddenly, there are signals from outer space. He's alive! More remarkably, he has the power of speech once more – whole sentences are tumbling out. The parents watch as his capsule bursts into earth's atmosphere. All their fears are over; their boy is back!

There were times when I thought Lloyd would never get back through the atmosphere, but he touched down when he was nineteen and has been a normal human being ever since.

P.S. Around the time when Lloyd (our non-compliant child) was fourteen, I prayed that God would allow me to live to the day when I could see him with a child of his own who wagged their finger, stamped their foot, shook their head and shouted, 'No!'

The other day I witnessed a conversation he was having at bedtime with his three-year-old son, Freddie. The small boy wagged his little finger, he stamped his little foot, he shook his little head, and he shouted, 'No!' As I watched them, I whispered under my breath, 'Sweet revenge, Son! Read my books!'

Sometimes during our events, people will ask me, 'How can you bear to share such personal details about your marriage in public?' The answer is that most of them aren't personal – they are the experience of the vast majority of the audience. As Dianne and I talk about our communication difficulties or moments of conflict, I see an expression on people's faces that says, 'That's just like us!' And when we begin to talk about some of the lessons we have learnt in the sexual arena, I hear sighs of relief from people as the realisation dawns that they are not the only ones wrestling with a particular problem, and I see them laugh – with us, and at themselves. Allow me to share a couple of 'personal' issues with you now.

The mystery of sex

I AM AMAZED HOW quickly Dianne can fall asleep some nights. She may see a slight twinkle in my eye and say, 'I'm going to bed, darling.' I tear up the stairs about three minutes behind her, but by the time I get to the bedroom Dianne is not only in bed but fast asleep. I walk noisily, I cough, I put my face right next to hers and whisper, 'I know that you can hear me!' But it's no use and I edge into bed only to hear Di mutter in her sleep, 'Good try, darling.'

And I am staggered at how often I misread the signs – even after so many years of married life. I remember one classic. It was our fifteenth wedding anniversary. I have booked a romantic restaurant. The big night comes, Di looks great, I am wearing the sweater she bought me for Christmas and I am plastered in an aftershave that guarantees that strange women will give you flowers in the street. It is obvious that, for this night at least, I have made myself irresistible.

We get to the restaurant; it is truly romantic. Candles are burning and in the background someone is playing a Spanish guitar. The fact that their choice of chords is limited to F, C and G7 can't dull the magic of this moment. As we are eating, I am thinking, 'Tonight is a certainty.' Gradually, as the thoughts take hold of my mind, I become impatient and say to Di, 'Are you ready for a dessert? Shall I get the bill?'

'Could I just finish the starter first?' she says patiently. After an eternity, we leave El Dorado's and wend our way home.

Once in the house, Dianne goes upstairs, but I think, 'I'll give her a moment or two', and linger downstairs for a while and apply further liberal splashings of aftershave. Finally, I enter the bedroom. She is walking towards me and has that long winceyette nightdress on with little roses and balls of fluff. She catches the look in my eye and says, 'Oh, you don't, do you?'

'Well,' I stutter, 'I did think, perhaps . . .'

The truth is that I didn't need the candles, the guitar, or the Spanish atmosphere to get me thinking about sex. I was thinking about it the day we put the date in the diary.

That would have been true of most men. But for Dianne the romance of the meal out together on our anniversary was enough in itself. I don't mean the shallow romance, but the real joy of being together in that setting without interruption; without anybody saying, 'There's a call for you', or, 'Can you come to . . .?', or, 'Mummy, where's my shoe?' For Dianne, the special evening (though not every such evening) didn't automatically have to lead to sex. I need to understand that, or I may feel rejected for no good reason.

P.S. Perhaps one day the shoe will be on the other foot and I will decide to say no. (Fat chance!)

Telling this story gives me the chance to quote from one of my favourite poems. The last line of it comes back to me time and time again: it has captured my heart.

Beds for all

I HAD THE INCREDIBLE privilege of being asked to speak at a carol service in the House of Commons a few years ago. It was held in the Speaker's Room, festively decorated with a huge Christmas tree standing in pride of place. Members of all political parties stood side by side in that most prestigious of buildings and sang 'Once in royal David's city stood a lowly cattle shed'.

When the service was over, I made my way out of Parliament. It was dark and the night was cold and crisp. I turned up the collar of my coat and began walking along Millbank. A man and woman were coming towards me; he was carrying a battered suitcase and she clutched a bundle of clothes tightly to her chest.

As we reached each other, the man asked me how to get

to St Martin-in-the-Fields Church. And then I understood. They were homeless and were trying to get to the place that has helped so many who had no bed for the night; it is known as 'the church of the ever-open door'. I said to them, 'It's not far. Just down this road, then across into Whitehall and on up to . . .' But then I paused. I think I felt overwhelmed by their sheer vulnerability on that winter's night. I stopped giving them directions and looked down the road. Within seconds, I saw the bright yellow light I had been hoping for. I hailed the cab, gave the couple a little money, and said to the driver, 'They want St Martin-in-the-Fields Church.'

The taxi moved away, and I watched as it went back past the Houses of Parliament and finally lost it to view as it turned left towards Trafalgar Square. But long after it was gone, I found myself still staring down the road. I felt as if the centuries had rolled away, and I had just witnessed a very old Christmas scene: a man and a woman in search of that most basic of human needs – a little warmth and a bed for the night. I was reminded of some lines from this lovely poem by Christina Rossetti:

Up-hill

Does the road wind up-hill all the way?
Yes, to the very end . . .

But is there for the night a resting-place?
A roof for when the slow dark hours begin.
May not the darkness hide it from my face?
You cannot miss that inn . . .

Shall I find comfort travel-sore and weak?
Of labour you shall find the sum.
Will there be beds for me and all who seek?
Yea, beds for all who come.

I have often wondered whether Mary told Jesus the story of the night he was born and how they were told, 'No room.' And I wonder whether that story was behind something Jesus said to his disciples the night before he died. He had just given them news that rocked their world: one of them would betray him, one would deny him and, perhaps worst of all, he would be leaving them. And then he said, 'Do not let your hearts be troubled . . . My Father's house has many rooms . . . I am going there to prepare a place for you.' It is as if, at the lowest moment of their lives, he wants them to grasp the reality and the security of that other world. At the end of their journey there will be a welcome: all will be well.

Sometimes I find myself feeling like the couple I met on that winter's night outside the Houses of Parliament

– tired and a little lost. At those times, I remind myself of Jesus' words and the reality of that final welcome. And it is then that I find myself whispering the words of the poet:

'Yea, beds for all who come.'

Our past is very strong. Sometimes we want to leave it behind, particularly when we're at a new stage in our lives – perhaps starting a new job or taking up a new opportunity – and especially when we're in a new relationship like marriage. But the past is usually not relinquished easily, and therefore, in some way or another, we have to deal with it; otherwise the ghosts of the past may come visiting. This is a story I tell about a young couple at the very beginning of their married life together.

When the past comes visiting

THEY HAVE JUST got back from their honeymoon, the confetti is hardly out of their hair, and the memory of all those cards being read aloud at the wedding reception is still alive in their brains. They wander around their new flat and into the spare room where all the presents that loving friends and family have given are waiting for them. Alongside the beautifully wrapped gifts are piles of personal belongings – the clutter of two lives.

So there they are: the old and the new possessions, all that this wide-eyed couple have to bring into their new life together. But wait. What are the two boxes over there, almost hidden in the dusty corner of the room? Where did they come from?

They are old, very old. The wood on each is worn with

age, scarred from use, the brass of the handles dull with neglect, and on both are labels dated with the very years that they were born. Who packed them so full that they could scarcely be lifted? And, having packed them, who brought them here, and what do they contain?

This man and woman, now husband and wife, will soon find the answers, for it was they themselves who packed the boxes – packed them piece by piece over twenty-five years, an entire life's history of emotions and experiences. Oh, the newlyweds did not intend to bring those old things to this new home, but the boxes would not be left behind and, unknowingly, they have dragged them, bumped them, over the threshold of their new life together. And there will come a time when the boxes will be opened and the contents – painful events, emotional scars, quiet expectations and well-used patterns of behaviour – will eventually be unpacked.

It was on a Tuesday night at seven o'clock when it first happened. He got in late from work and the table was already laid. They chatted as she served the meal. What he said next was not vicious or vindictive, nor even premeditated. He said, 'I think I'll have mine in the other room on a tray – there's a match on the television.'

The lasagne missed him because he ducked. 'What did I say?' he muttered as she stormed out. How could he have known that as he declared his simple intention to watch the match tonight, the box belonging to his wife would open? Her mind would flash back fifteen years and a memory would come flooding back. She would remember a man sitting in front of the television with his meal on a tray. She would see clearly, as though she were there again, her mother trying to share some incident of the day with this man, a man who remained silent. And she would hear a little girl asking him to play with her – and the old reply, 'Yes – later.'

Oh, they will make it up, this young couple. And she will say, 'I'm sorry – that was silly.' But it was not silly, for none of us walks through life with our box empty. We each have one and we carry it around with us from encounter to encounter, relationship to relationship – and, of course, into marriage. Sadly, many of us don't even know it's there. All we *do* know is that we seem to react to certain circumstances in a particular way – but we couldn't begin to guess why. The lid is thrown open, and both big and small issues are pulled out: how we respond to praise, react to a petty argument, or even how we behave behind the wheel of a car.

The old baggage can drag us down, but it needn't. We can clear some of that old stuff out and gain insights into the ways we react to situations that are hurtful to those around us. None of this is easy. It requires patience, understanding and a willingness to change. It means stopping ourselves long enough to ask, 'Why am I feeling this way?' 'Why am I saying these things?' And when we've done that, we must learn to be honest with our partners about our past hurts, heartbreaks and disappointments.

Otherwise, one day, a ghost may come visiting.

I once saw a dramatic illustration of the awesome power of a parent to create a negative sense of value in a child. When I first met her, Emily, a single woman, was in her forties. She was painfully reserved. When she did speak, it was often with a biting tongue and she would respond to questions with a grunt. She dressed in a way to make herself look not only unattractive but at least fifteen years older than her actual age. She walked with a slight stoop. But Emily was something of an enigma; that sullen, unattractive face held the most incredible eyes.

The wrong kind of love

EMILY NEVER DRANK alcohol, which perhaps explained what occurred at a friend's party. Very simply, she thought the punch was non-alcoholic; it wasn't. After she'd drunk two glasses, she sat next to me and did something I'd never known her do before: she began to talk like a normal person. There was none of the usual sarcasm about other guests or the standard of the food. Emily looked as if she was too weary for all that and a wistful look came into her eyes instead. She began to tell me about her childhood.

Her father had died when she was nine, but her memories of him were good ones. He would often come home from work, sweep her into his arms and tell her he loved her. If he was late and she had already gone to sleep, he would slip into her bedroom and sit on the end of her bed. She remembers stirring sometimes and saying sleepily, 'Hello, Daddy. What are you doing here?' His reply was always the same: 'I'm watching you and thinking how beautiful you are.' And then he would tuck the blankets around her, straighten the top sheet and sit there, silently. Emily never felt more secure in the whole of her life, knowing that even as she slipped back into sleep, he was there.

I had been put down by Emily so often that I was scared of saying the wrong thing, but I risked it: 'You must miss him.' I don't know what I expected her to say. I suppose it was anything except, 'When he died, a part of me did too.'

'Why do you say that?'

She rummaged in her handbag and produced a black and white photograph. I gazed into the eyes of one of the most beautiful teenage girls I have ever seen. She took it from me.

'I was lovely, yes?'

'More than that,' I said, '. . . utterly beautiful. But why do you say a part of you died when you lost your father?'

'Because my mother loved me with the wrong kind of love.'

'What do you mean?'

She sighed: 'When somebody loves you with the wrong kind of love you can never please them. When you do badly, they get cross and can't wait to tell you where you went wrong. When you do well, it simply reminds them you could be even better if you tried harder, so you never hear they are pleased with you. And after a while, unless you are very strong, you become the person they think you are and the real person dies. My father saw all the good in me and couldn't stop talking about it; my mother always wanted me to be better than I was. Her love only wanted to change me. If I came in the top ten at school, she'd tell me that if I worked harder I'd be in the top five. She told me my skin was poor because I didn't get enough fresh air, and my hair was thin because I didn't eat enough fish. Once, when I was sixteen, I saved for three months for a dress to wear to the end-of-term ball. When I came downstairs in it, she told me it made me look cheap. I went to my room, sat on my bed and cut it into little strips.'

'Is she still alive?' I asked.

'No, she died five years ago. Her last words to me were, "Your glasses are on crooked."'

For my money, no piece of writing, academic or otherwise, describes so succinctly as the following little piece[11] the essence of a being just two years old, three feet tall, and with the determination of Attila the Hun.

A toddler's property laws

If I like it, it's mine.

If it's in my hand, it's mine.

If I can take it from you, it's mine.

If I had it a little while ago, it's mine.

If it's mine, it must never appear to be yours in any way.

If I'm doing or building something, all the pieces are
mine.

If it looks just like mine, it's mine.

If I saw it first, it's mine.

If you are playing with something and you put it down,
it automatically becomes mine.

If it's broken, it's yours.

After I wrote Bringing Home the Prodigals, *I went on a speaking tour that took me all over the world. At the end of each event, there would often be a line of people waiting to speak to me or to pray with me for their prodigals to come home. I heard the most incredible stories during those times, both from parents and from the prodigals themselves.*

Always leave a light on

I WROTE ONE OF my books in a small conference centre on the Gower coast. The building is set on a hill and the view from my window was unspeakably beautiful, running across fields, then woods and finally ending at the sea in the great sweep of Oxwich Bay. One morning, I took a break from writing and stood outside the house gazing into the distance at the breakers hitting the beach. After a few minutes, I was joined by a priest. He wore the traditional long black cassock and had a flowing grey beard. He had been leading a discussion in one of the seminar rooms and said he'd just popped out to get some air.

We began chatting and he asked me what I was doing. When I told him I was writing a book about prodigals

– those who seemed to have wandered away from their faith – he told me a moving story. Let me try to capture his words:

> In a village near here, is a large old house. An elderly lady lives there alone, and every night, as darkness falls, she puts a light on in the attic. Her son left home twenty-five years ago, rather like the prodigal in the parable, but she has never given up the hope that one day he will come home. We all know the house well, and although the bulb must occasionally need replacing, none of us have ever seen that house without a light on. It is for her son.

Since then, I've spoken about prodigals many times and I always tell that story. After one such occasion, I received a letter from a woman who had been in the audience. She said that when her daughter was eighteen she had walked out of their home after a row. She didn't get in touch, and they didn't know whether she was alive or dead. At night, as this mother and her husband turned off the lights before they went to bed, she would always say to him, 'Leave the porch light on.' And every Christmas she would put a little Christmas tree in the front of the house, its lights shining, just as she used to when her daughter was a child.

That couple didn't see their daughter for six years. Then one day, out of the blue, she knocked on their door and fell into her mother's arms. She said: 'Mum, I so often wanted to come home, but I was too ashamed. Sometimes, though, in the early hours of the morning, I would drive my car into our street and just sit there. I used to gaze at the houses and every one of them was dark apart from our house: you always left a light on. And at Christmas I would do the same: just sit there in the darkness and look at the Christmas tree you had put outside – I knew it was for me.'

I have said these words to parents all over the world:

'Don't ever give up hope . . . keep on praying . . . and always leave a light on.'

The strange thing about getting older is that while you can't remember where you left your glasses, you can recall events from your childhood with stunning clarity. Sometimes it's difficult to work out why those experiences win the fight over a million others to gain such a prominent place in our minds, but I don't find it at all hard to understand why the memories I will share with you now are two of the most vivid from my schooldays.

When your best isn't good enough

I WASN'T GOOD AT school, not academically nor even at practical subjects – a double blow in the confidence arena. When I was fourteen, the teacher in my woodwork class at school told us that for that term's final exam we could make either a coffee table or a potato plunger. I don't blame you for not knowing what a potato plunger is – neither did I – nor care, until I saw how complicated the coffee table looked. A potato plunger is used to, well . . . plunge. It makes a big hole in the ground into which you insert . . . a potato.

I gave that potato plunger everything I had and finally I laid it on the bench waiting for the teacher to walk around and inspect our work. He passed the other kids' work, coffee table after coffee table. When he reached me, he looked at my offering, sniffed, and said, 'What is it?' I remember thinking how unfair that was – it obviously wasn't the coffee table.

'Sir,' I said, 'it's a potato plunger.'

He replied, 'It's awful.'

I said, 'I did my best.'

And then he said, 'Parsons – your best is not good enough.'

I have often thought about his reply. Where do you go in life as a fourteen-year-old boy when your best isn't good enough?

When it comes to feeling valued, children are all too aware how the system works. In school the honours are given to those at the top of the academic pecking order; in sport they know that the kids who break the tape first get the silver cups; and with regard to their friends, it's the best-looking who get the boyfriends and girlfriends first. But children with a sense of their own value have the incredible foundation in life of being able to say, 'My parents accept me.' That doesn't mean their mother and father don't encourage them to do better at school or that they wouldn't prefer them to be more willing to help with the washing-up. It certainly doesn't mean that their parents approve of their every action. But it does mean that a child knows that at the bottom of it all, at least with their mother and father, they are accepted for who they are and are therefore loved.

Sometimes, especially with the apparently less able child, we have to find a little encouragement where we can. My woodwork teacher could have learnt a few lessons in that area from Mr Thomas, my primary school teacher. I was nine years old when he asked me to come to the front of the class and hold the paper for the guillotine. These sheets were used for our drawing and painting and Mr Thomas was very particular that each had a perfectly straight edge. I had never been asked to have any responsibility before, yet alone been at the front of the class, and even now I remember leaving my desk and with great trepidation making my way to the front.

I gave Mr Thomas a great edge that day – so much so that the following week he did something he had never done before and asked the *same* boy to hold the paper again. And he asked me again on the third week and the fourth week. On the fifth week, as I made my way back to my desk having performed the task yet again, Mr Thomas said, 'Robert Parsons is the best holder of guillotine paper in the whole of the class.'

Let me share a secret with you: as I typed this story up, my eyes filled with tears. How strange. I have told this story so many times, but I think it was because I could see again with stunning clarity the moment that little boy made his way to the front of the class on that first occasion, and even feel the fear that he would mess up the opportunity he had been given.

Since making that short walk, I have had an interesting life with many incredible opportunities, but 'Robert Parsons is the best holder of guillotine paper in the whole of the class' still has a special place in my heart. And I think it's because when your self-esteem is pretty low and somebody praises you for something – no matter how small – you get the scent of a possibility that there could be bigger victories out there.

It was late on a Sunday evening that it happened. I had taken a group of teenagers on a beach barbeque, but as they leapt from the cars to run to the sand, one child lingered in the car. If only we had some warning of life-changing events, perhaps we could get ready in some way for them, but that is not in their nature; such moments surprise us, sneak up on us, ambush us. It was so on this occasion.

I know where I'm going

THE GIRL WHO stayed behind in the car with me as the rest of the youth group ran down to the beach was fifteen, and within six months she would be dead. When she was fourteen, Alicia contracted cancer. The chemotherapy had caused her hair to fall out, and when I sat with her that night it was just beginning to grow back. We could hear the sounds of shouts and screams in the distance as a typical youth group argued over who had found the largest piece of driftwood, but at that moment it was quiet in my car. I fumbled for something to say before asking, 'Alicia, how are you coping with all this?'

And it was then that she said it. She had no idea what she was about to do. It did not enter her head that her words would be broadcast across the world, that radio and television would beam them to places she had never heard of. She did not know that men and women would catch their breath when they heard them; that people who had lost hope would be lifted in spirit.

I last spoke her words on the stage of the Waterfront Hall in Belfast, one of the finest concert halls in the world, in front of a packed audience. The spotlights were in my eyes and I couldn't make out the faces in the front row, let alone the thousands of others reaching right up into the gods. But I imagined the looks on people's faces, sensed the emotion, and caught a little of the hope as I shouted her words into the darkness:

'Alicia Owens said: "I know where I'm going."'

She was just fifteen and you may think her naïve, but I don't. You may say, 'She had no idea of the pain ahead.' But she had already suffered much; she knew what lay before her. No, her words were not born out of shallowness or immaturity. Alicia was looking the greatest enemy in the face and saying in her heart, 'You are not as fearsome as I first thought. You cannot hold me.'

As I drove home later that night, her words did not leave me. In fact, I think I knew even then that they never would. Alicia knew what kings and presidents do not know. She knew where she was going.

Some months after our conversation in the car and as Alicia lay very near to death, I held her hand and told her

I was going to dedicate the book that I had just written, called *The Sixty Minute Father*, to her. I said, 'It will be to Alicia Owens – who knew where she was going.' She was pleased and smiled, and I was honoured to do it, but neither of us had any idea that all over the globe people would ask me to tell the story of that teenager's faith and her certainty in a world more real than this.

Shortly after she died, I was asked to speak on the BBC and I told listeners about Alicia and read something that seemed to capture the heart of her belief. It talks of death in terms of passing over the horizon.

Gone From My Sight

I am standing upon the seashore.
A ship at my side spreads her white sails to the morning
breeze
and starts for the blue ocean.
She is an object of beauty and strength,
and I stand and watch until at last she hangs
like a speck of white cloud
just where the sea and sky come down to mingle with
each other.
Then someone at my side says,
'There! She's gone!'

Gone where?

Gone from my sight . . . that is all.
She is just as large in mast and hull and spar
as she was when she left my side
and just as able to bear her load of living freight
to the place of destination.
Her diminished size is in me, not in her.
And just at the moment
when someone at my side says,
'There! She's gone!'
there are other eyes watching her coming . . .
and other voices ready to take up the glad shout . . .

'Here she comes!'[13]

I love this story. It has everything: a snowy Canadian valley, an old recluse, and a kid who's scared of being eaten alive!

Bearer of hope

BRUCE, A FRIEND of mine, has a wonderful Christmas memory from when he was a boy. He was born in Northern Ontario, Canada, where the winters are traditionally cold and snowy. His home was an isolated farm, deep in the heart of the country. Several miles further on was a dwelling that enjoyed even greater isolation. It was inhabited by an old recluse called Joe. If anybody wanted to visit Joe (and most people didn't!) they had better be ready for a trek through the woods. Apparently Joe was something of a local mystery – most adults found it easier to ignore him and most kids were in awe of him. Wild stories were passed from child to child about the number of kids Joe had eaten alive, and rumour had it that if he caught you within a mile of his place you would disappear for ever.

Every Christmas, Bruce's father, Don, would trudge through the woods to Joe's cottage to give him some Christmas gifts and, as he put it, 'to let the old boy know that somebody cares'.

Bruce told me he could remember what happened on Christmas Eve 1958 as though it was yesterday. The night before, new snow had blanketed their valley and then the weather had turned clear and cold. Bruce had shivered as he came downstairs and found his father making breakfast beside the old stove. His dad turned to him and said, 'In a moment I'm going to make my trip to Joe's place. Would you like to come with me? I'm carrying quite a bit and I'd appreciate the help.' Bruce said it was hard to believe that his own father wanted him to be eaten alive, but he was torn – no child had ever visited the cottage. He said he'd go.

They walked for thirty minutes or so, their boots making fresh prints in the virgin snow, and then his father pointed to a thin wisp of smoke curling up from the centre of the wood. They waded through knee-deep snowdrifts and, finally, panting and exhausted, knocked on Joe's door. Bruce's heart was pounding in his chest.

The door was opened not by a monster but by an old man with holes in his clothes and a gruff voice that welcomed them in. They entered a one-roomed house that had seen better days and was filled with the smell of a hardwood fire and the unmistakable waft of body odour and old tobacco. Bruce's father set the bags of groceries they'd hauled through the snow onto a sticky oilcloth-covered table near where Joe invited them to sit.

Bruce watched, wide-eyed, while the men made small talk, discussing the recent turn in the weather and whether there would be enough wood to last the winter. After all the local topics had been well covered, Bruce's father said, 'Well, Christmas is here again and our family just wanted you to have a few groceries as our gift to you. Merry Christmas, Joe!'

And then Bruce's young eyes saw something he has never forgotten. A single tear began to roll down Joe's face and into his thick bushy beard. The old recluse brushed it away with the back of a dirty hand as he mumbled his thanks.

It was the last Christmas Eve journey they made to Joe. He died the following January.

Bruce told me that when he looks back at that day so many years ago, one thing especially stands out in his mind: just as they were about to leave the cottage, Joe reached out, touched Don's arm and said, 'Don, you are a bearer of hope.'

I believe that one of the greatest barriers to keeping relationships – and families – together is the modern idea that love is just a feeling. Couples say to me, 'We're breaking up; we don't feel in love any more.' When I'm faced with people, particularly young people, who say that's how they are feeling, I tell them this story that has touched the hearts of thousands across the world. It is an incident recounted by Dr Richard Selzer.[14]

Proving the kiss still works

I stand by the bed where a young woman lies, her face post-operative, her mouth twisted in palsy, clownish. A tiny twig of the facial nerve, the one to the muscles of her mouth, has been severed. She will be thus from now on. The surgeon has followed with religious fervour the curve of her flesh; I promise you that. Nevertheless, to remove the tumour in her cheek, I had to cut the little nerve.

Her young husband is in the room. He stands on the opposite side of the bed, and together they seem to dwell in the evening lamplight, isolated from me, private. Who are they, I ask myself, he and this wry-mouth that I have made, who gaze at and touch each other so greedily? The young woman speaks.

'Will my mouth always be like this?' she asks.

'Yes,' I say, 'it will. It is because the nerve was cut.'

She nods, and is silent. But the young man smiles. 'I like it,' he says. 'It is kind of cute.'

All at once I *know* who he is. I understand, and I lower my gaze . . . Unmindful, he bends to kiss her crooked mouth, and I so close, I can see how he twists his own lips to accommodate hers, to show her that their kiss still works. I remember that the gods appeared in ancient Greece as mortals, and I hold my breath and let the wonder in.

There may come a time for many of us when our partner becomes unattractive to us for a while – perhaps physically, mentally, emotionally or intellectually. At such a time, love does not rise easily in our hearts. It is rather that from the very depths of our spirits, almost as an act of the will, we love against the odds.

We are altering the shape of our lips to prove the kiss still works.

There was a knock on our front door. Such a simple thing . . . but it was enough to change three lives for ever.

Somebody at the gate

ONE NIGHT JUST before Christmas, when Dianne and I been married for just a couple of years, there was a knock on our door. When I opened it, a man was standing there in the darkness. He was holding a frozen chicken in one hand and a black plastic bag in the other, which we later discovered contained all his worldly possessions.

I thought I recognised him. His name was Ron and when we were kids he used to come to our Sunday school. He was slightly educationally challenged and lived in a children's home. Every Sunday, Mr Harker, our Sunday school superintendent, used to collect Ron from the children's home and bring him to the little church on the corner of my street. Now he was in his late twenties. I said, 'It's Ron, isn't it.' He nodded. 'How did you know where we live?' He started to explain, but then I stopped him talking and simply invited him in. Ron had fallen on very hard times. I am sure that those who looked after him in the children's home had done their best for him; nevertheless, at the age of sixteen he'd had to leave and try to make his way in the world with almost no support and few skills – social or otherwise. He was now living in appalling conditions.

'Where did you get your frozen chicken, Ron?' I asked him. He told us that somebody had given it to him as a Christmas present. 'Do you know how to cook it?' I asked. He shook his head vigorously. Dianne took the chicken from his hands and said, 'I'll cook it – and why don't you stay with us tonight?' We found him some pyjamas and basic stuff and settled him into our spare room. He stayed with us the next night as well and the night after that. On the third day Dianne said, 'It's Christmas Eve, Ron. Don't leave tonight.'

On Christmas Day Ron joined us for lunch with a few other family members (this was before we had children). We had hastily wrapped a few presents for him, and he shared in the distribution of gifts when the meal was over. He cried. He had never known a family Christmas.

That day was forty years ago, and since then we've had two children. They are grown and gone now with children of their own, but Ron has never left us and, short of needing more care than we are able to give him, he never will. When he'd been with us a short time, he got a job as a dustman. In those days, I was a young lawyer, and on the way to the office I would drop Ron off for work at the dustyard. When I got home in the evening, Ron would often be sitting in the same chair, smiling away to himself. One night I asked him what it was that amused him so much. He said, 'When you drop me off at work in the mornings, the other men say, "Who's that who brings you to work in the car?" and I say, "Oh, that's my solicitor!"'

I have thought so much about that smile of Ron's. It wasn't that he was being driven to work by a lawyer (who'd be proud of that?). No, I think what was giving Ron so much joy went far deeper than that. He had never had a mum lead him by the hand into the playground on his first day of school. He had never had a dad say, when he was eleven, 'How was your first day in the big school, Son?' And now he was a man – but, for the first time ever, *somebody was at the gate*.

Life can be hard for any of us. I remember sitting on a train in the New York subway some years ago. My fellow passengers and I had our heads sunk in our newspapers and looked up only briefly when a young man, who appeared as though he had been sleeping rough, began making a pitch for money. But suddenly he stopped asking us to open our wallets and said, 'Ladies and gentlemen, I haven't always been like this. And you should all know that anything can happen to anybody.'

As I glanced around the carriage, I saw that people had lifted their heads from the sports or fashion pages and were looking intently at him. And I know why. We didn't just have a homeless man trying to raise a little cash in our carriage – we had a philosopher on the train. And in our hearts, we all knew that he was right: *anything can happen to anybody*.

People sometimes ask me, 'Why do we need charities like Care for the Family?' My answer is always the same and it's twofold:

Because anything can happen to anybody.

And because we all need somebody at the gate.

Planning for the future

THIS BOOK IS part of Care for the Family's thirtieth anniversary celebrations. We are a national charity that works to strengthen and support family life. When the charity began, it was just Dianne and me, a part-time secretary, and a friend helping when he could. We now have over eighty staff, offices across the United Kingdom, and, by God's grace, we have been able to touch the lives of millions of people.

A couple of years ago, a woman approached me during the interval at one of our evening parenting events. She said, 'When I was a little girl, your books used to be on my parents' bookshelves and then their marriage went through a difficult period and they were helped by watching your *Marriage Matters* video.' (I remember filming that in the Wembley Conference Centre in 1991.) She continued, 'When I got married, they gave us a copy of *The Sixty Minute Marriage* book and then a little later we were having a tough time in our relationship and we watched your *21st Century Marriage* DVD. We came through that time and now my husband and I run Care for the Family's marriage courses to help other couples.'

I felt about 112!

My hope is for Care for the Family to go on touching lives for another thirty years and beyond – not just for the sake of *our* children, but for our children's children. When we strengthen family life, we affect the very foundation of our society and change all our tomorrows for good.

From your first experience as a parent, we'll be there for you as you go through the sleepless nights, the teething, and the toddler tantrums. When you hold your child's hand on their first day at school, we'll hold yours. We'll support you through the primary years and help prepare both you and your children to navigate the big issues of the teenage years. And you can get in touch if you are struggling with the empty nest (one mum wrote about her son and said, 'He went to college and suddenly I walked past *a too-tidy* bedroom').

If you have a child with additional needs, we'll put you in touch with one of our befrienders – parents who have walked that path before you, caring for their own children with additional needs. If tragedy strikes and you lose a child, our bereaved parents team will stand alongside you. If you are a single parent, we'll be there for you and help you keep going in that most challenging of roles.

If you are married and your relationship is strong, we want to help strengthen it even more in those good times. If you hit trouble in your relationship, we will try to help you come through. And if your family breaks up for any reason, we will be there for you. If you suffer the tragedy of losing a partner early in life, a dedicated team, all of whom have themselves been widowed, will offer you support and try, above all, to give you hope.

Do check us out on our website (www.cff.org.uk) and don't hesitate to get in touch if you think we can be of help. Thousands of people have attended our events and courses, and we have been privileged to be able to offer them encouragement and support. Over the years, people have told me repeatedly that our books, DVDs, an event or other resources have made a real difference to them and their family.

I am so grateful for the work we have been able to do in the past, but I am reminded of something Mark Twain said: 'Plan for the future because that's where you are going to spend the rest of your life'. It is on the families – and especially the children – of the future that our vision is now fixed. If you feel you could support us financially in some way, we would be so grateful. Perhaps you could even consider leaving us a legacy in your will to help us continue bringing help and encouragement to future generations.

I really hope you have enjoyed reading this book, but as much as that, I hope that you'll get the chance to attend one of our live events. You'll be sitting among hundreds of people, perhaps four rows back from the stage, the lights will go down, and I promise you that sometime very shortly after we start, you'll hear me say . . .

'Let me tell you a story.'

Notes

1. Adapted from 'Appointment with Love' by S. I. Kishor, Collier's Weekly, 1943.
2. Adapted from 'The voice in the Box' by Paul Villard, Reader's Digest, 1966.
3. Harry and Sandra Chapin, 'Cat's in the Cradle'.
4. Adapted from 'The Animal School' by George H. Reavis, 1940.
5. Ecclesiastes 4:4.
6. Henri Nouwen, *The Genesee Diary*, Bantam Doubleday Dell, revised edition, 1989.
7. 1 Corinthians 15:52–53.
8. Adapted from 'Johnny Lingo and the Eight-Cow Wife' by Patricia McGerr, *Woman's Day*, November 1965.
9. Psalm 139:8–10, NIV.
10. Adapted from Colin Bowles, *The Beginner's Guide to Fatherhood*, Angus & Robertson, 1992.
11. Allan Ahlberg, *Please Mrs Butler*, Puffin, 1984.
12. Author unknown.
13. Revd Luther F. Beecher (1813–1903).
14. R. Seltzer, *Mortal Lessons: Notes on the Art of Surgery*, New York: Simon & Schuster, 1976.

Care for the Family is a national charity
which aims to promote strong family life
and to help those who face family difficulties.
A snapshot of what we do includes events,
networks, online and other resources to support:

• Parents • Couples
• Families with additional needs
• Bereaved parents • Young widows/widowers
• Single parents

Care for the Family
mail@cff.org.uk
029 2081 0800

If you would like to support the work of
Care for the Family, visit our website at
cff.org.uk/donate
for further information.

You can keep in touch by subscribing to our newsletter
or following us on Facebook, Twitter or Instagram.